GERMANY

A GEOGRAPHIC COLORING BOOK

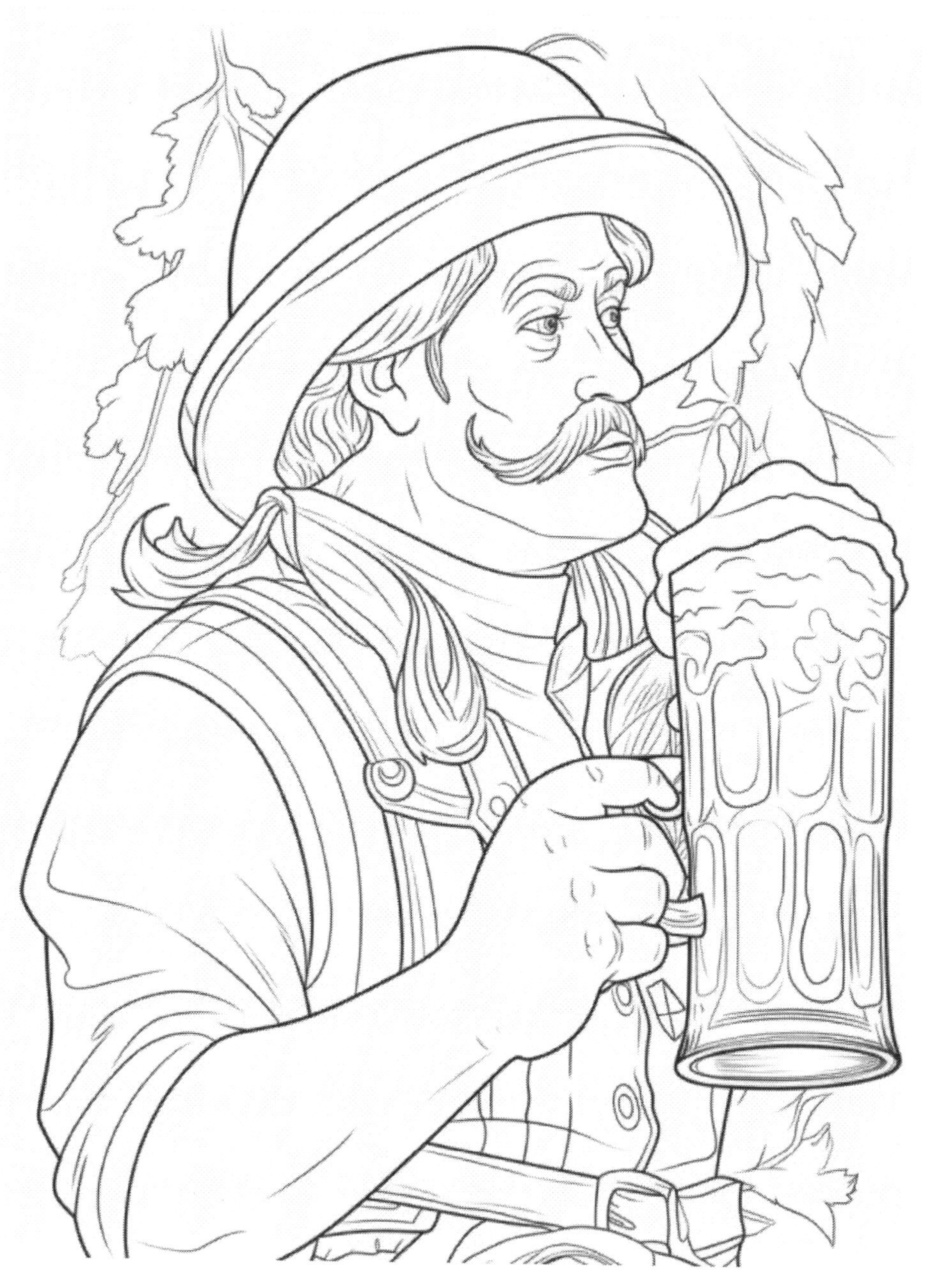

BY JOEL LEWIS

ISBN: 9798396340473

THIS BOOK
BELONGS TO:

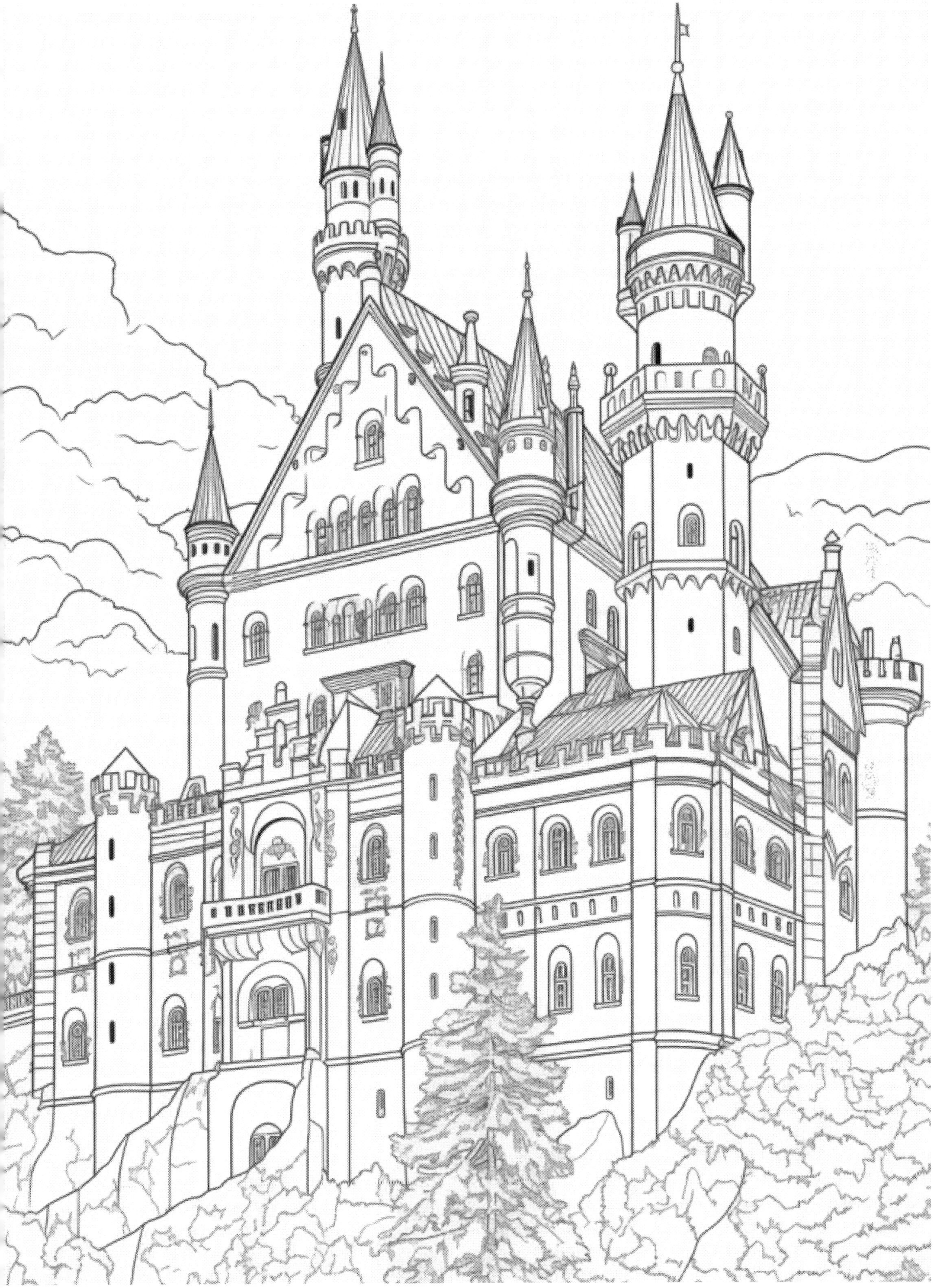

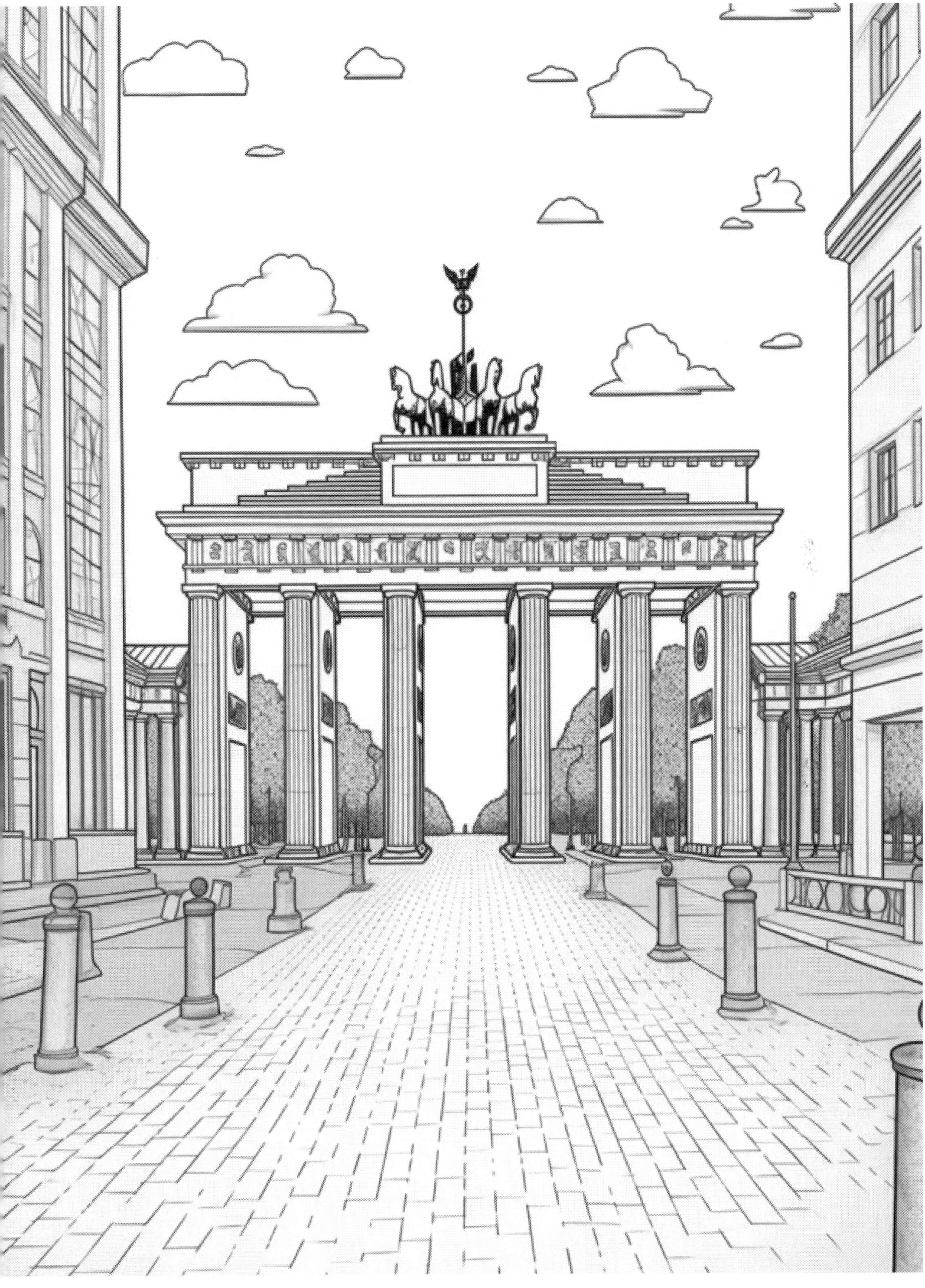

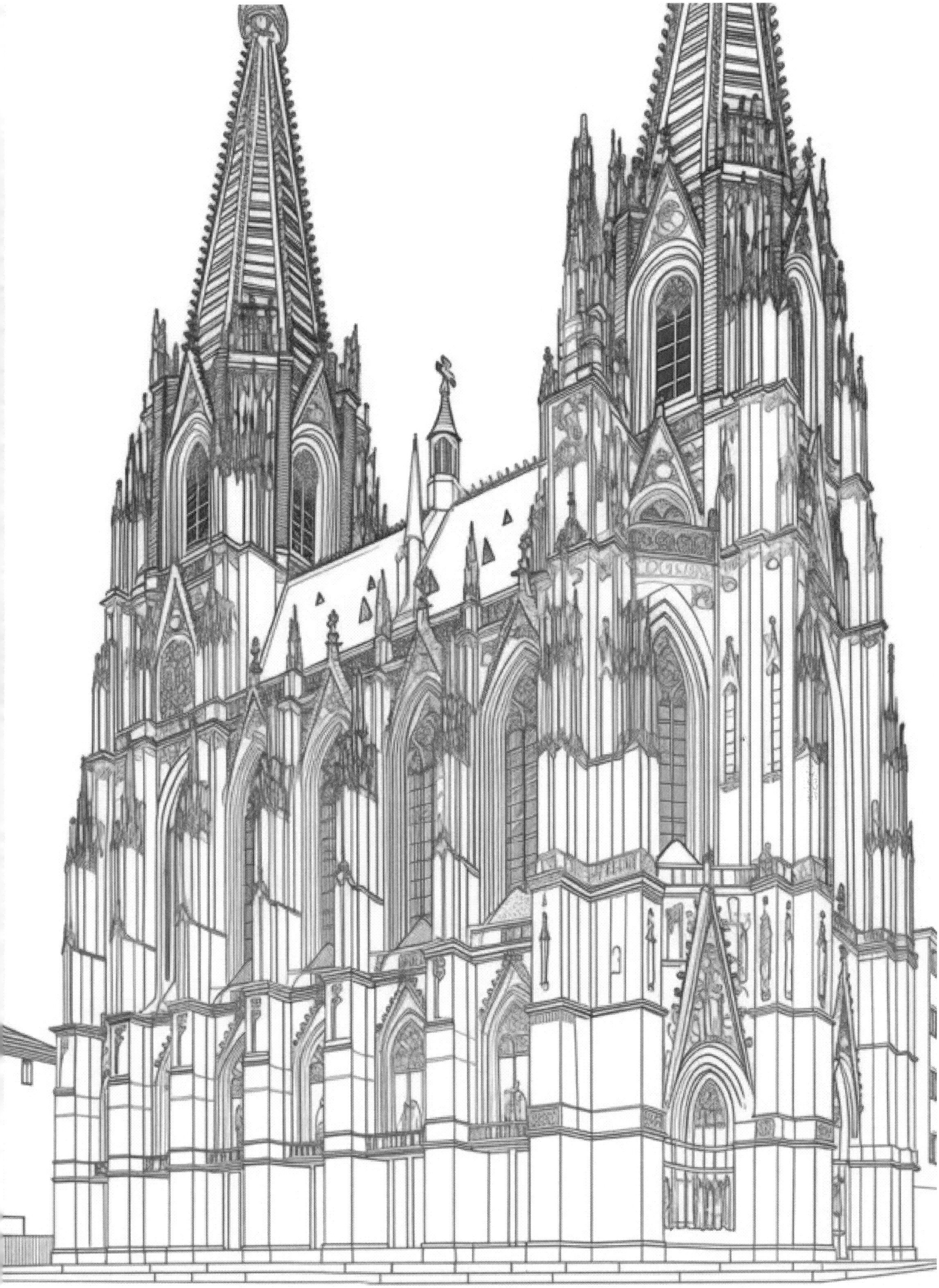

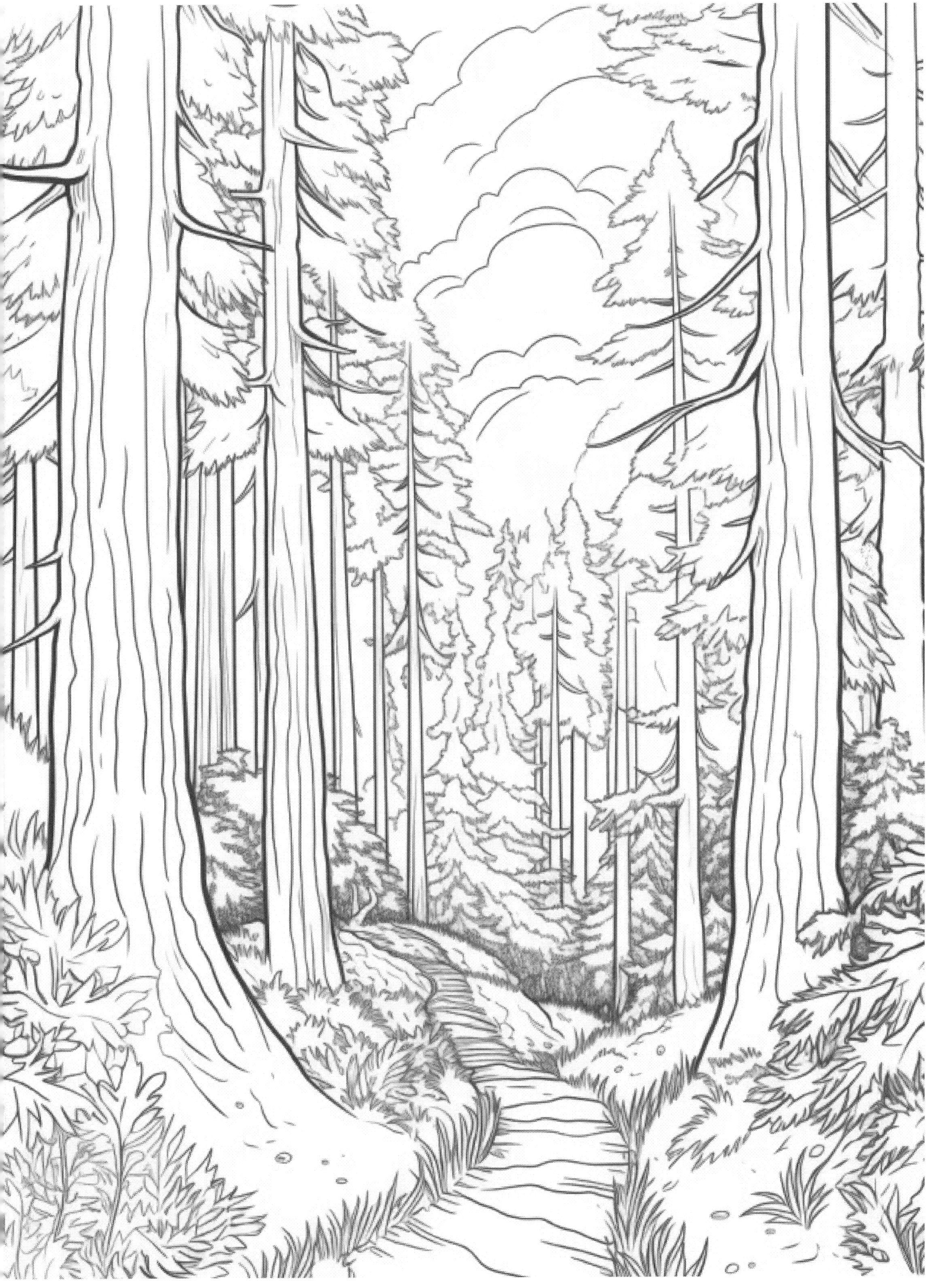

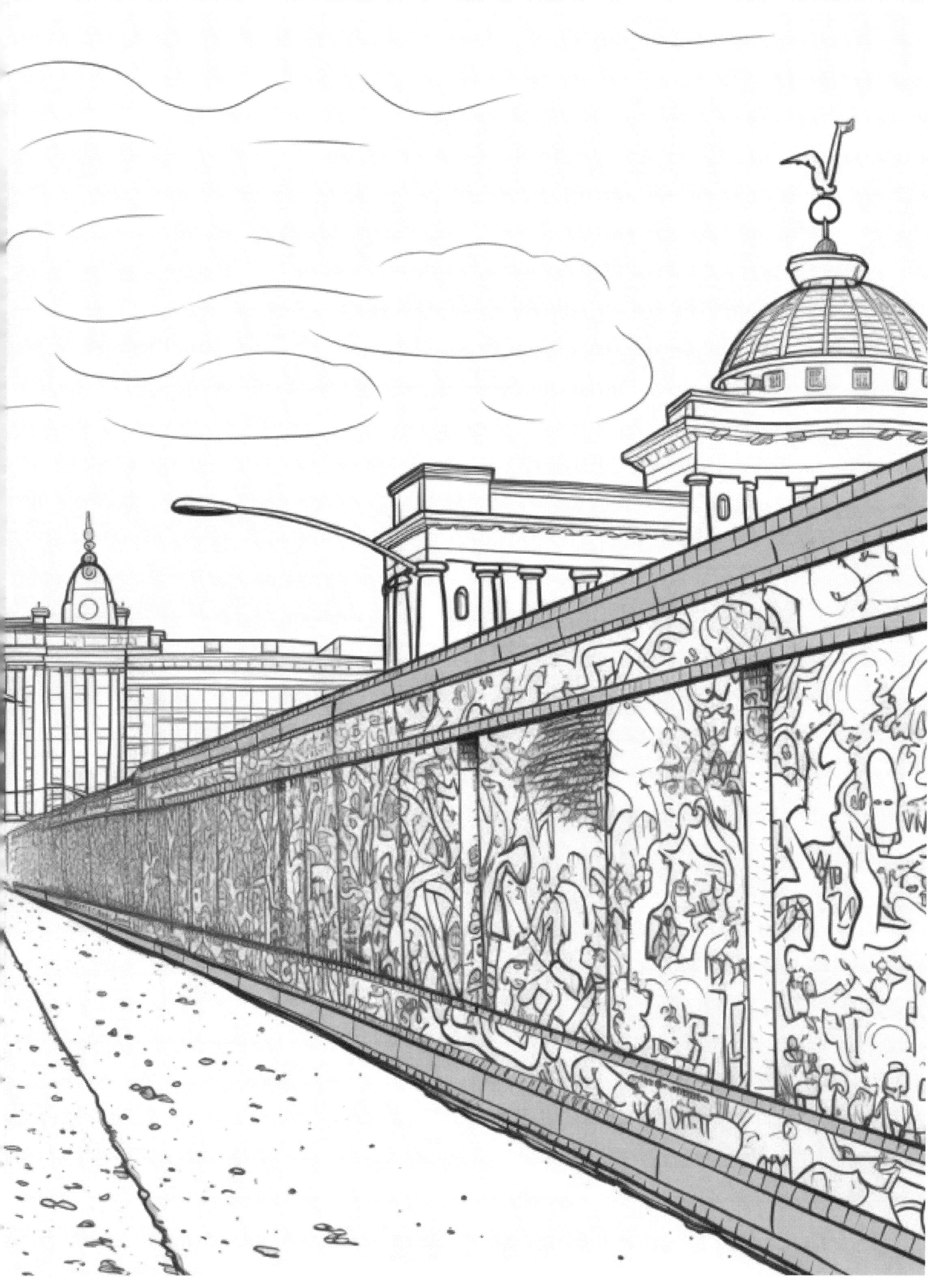

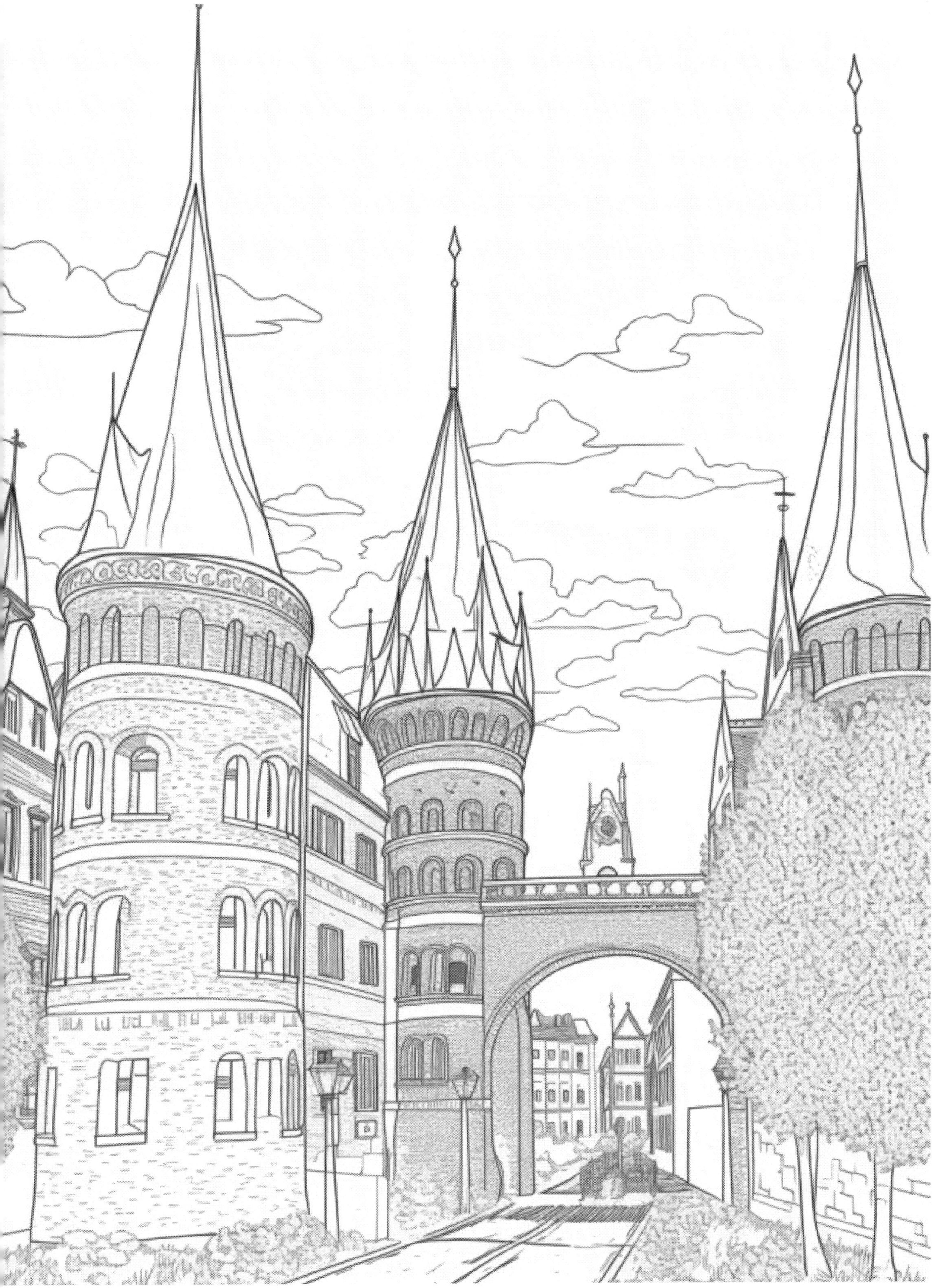

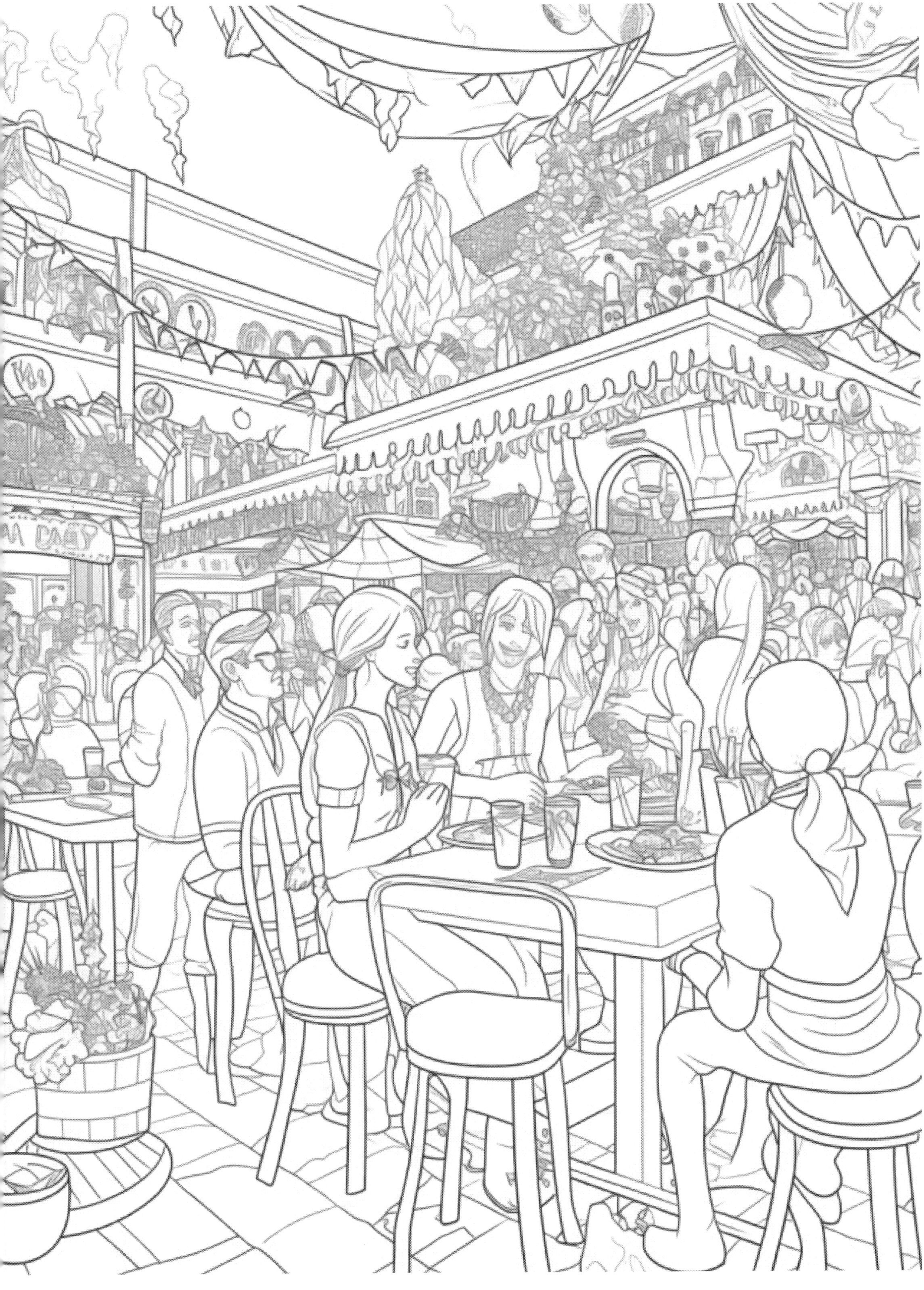

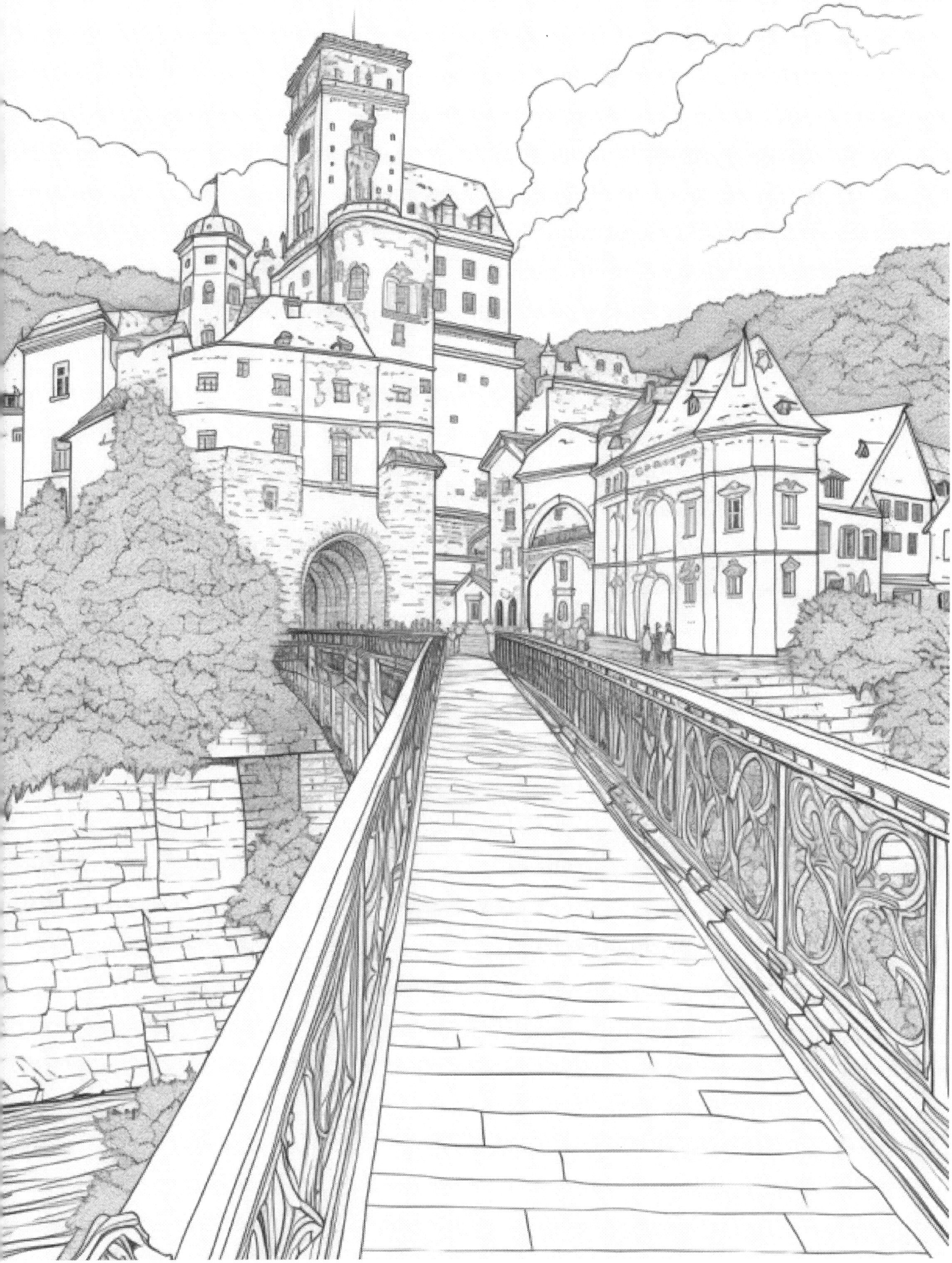

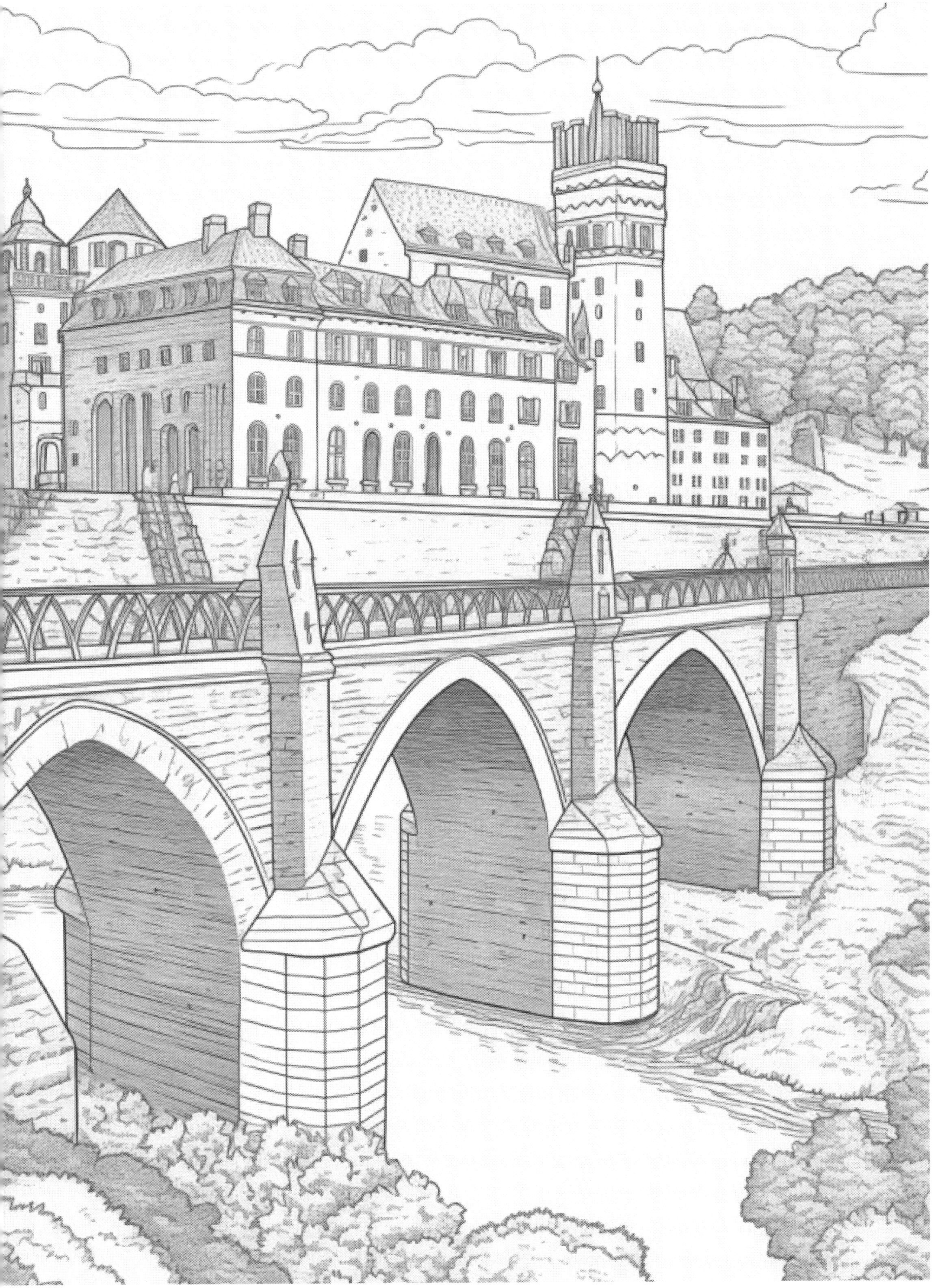

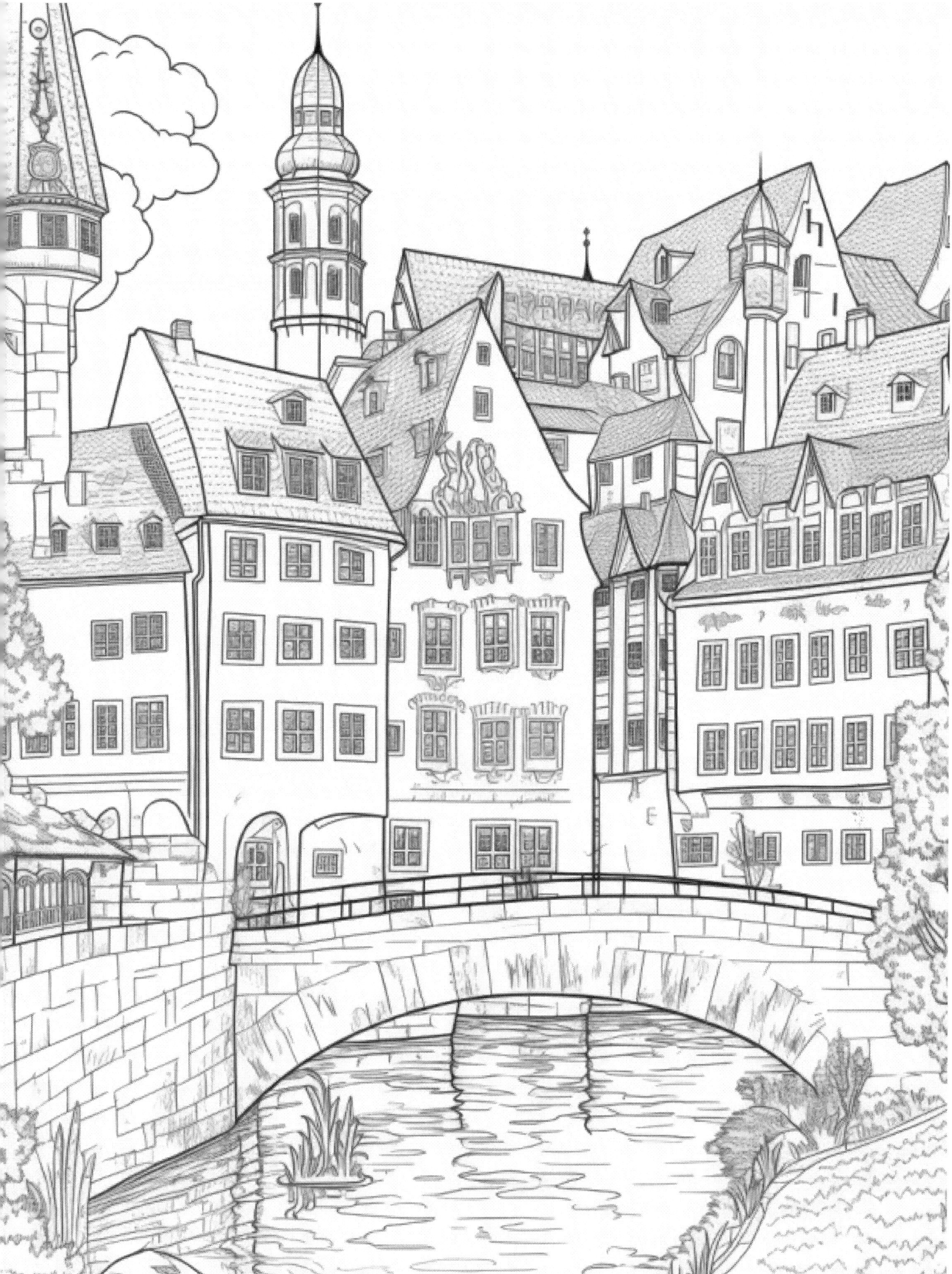

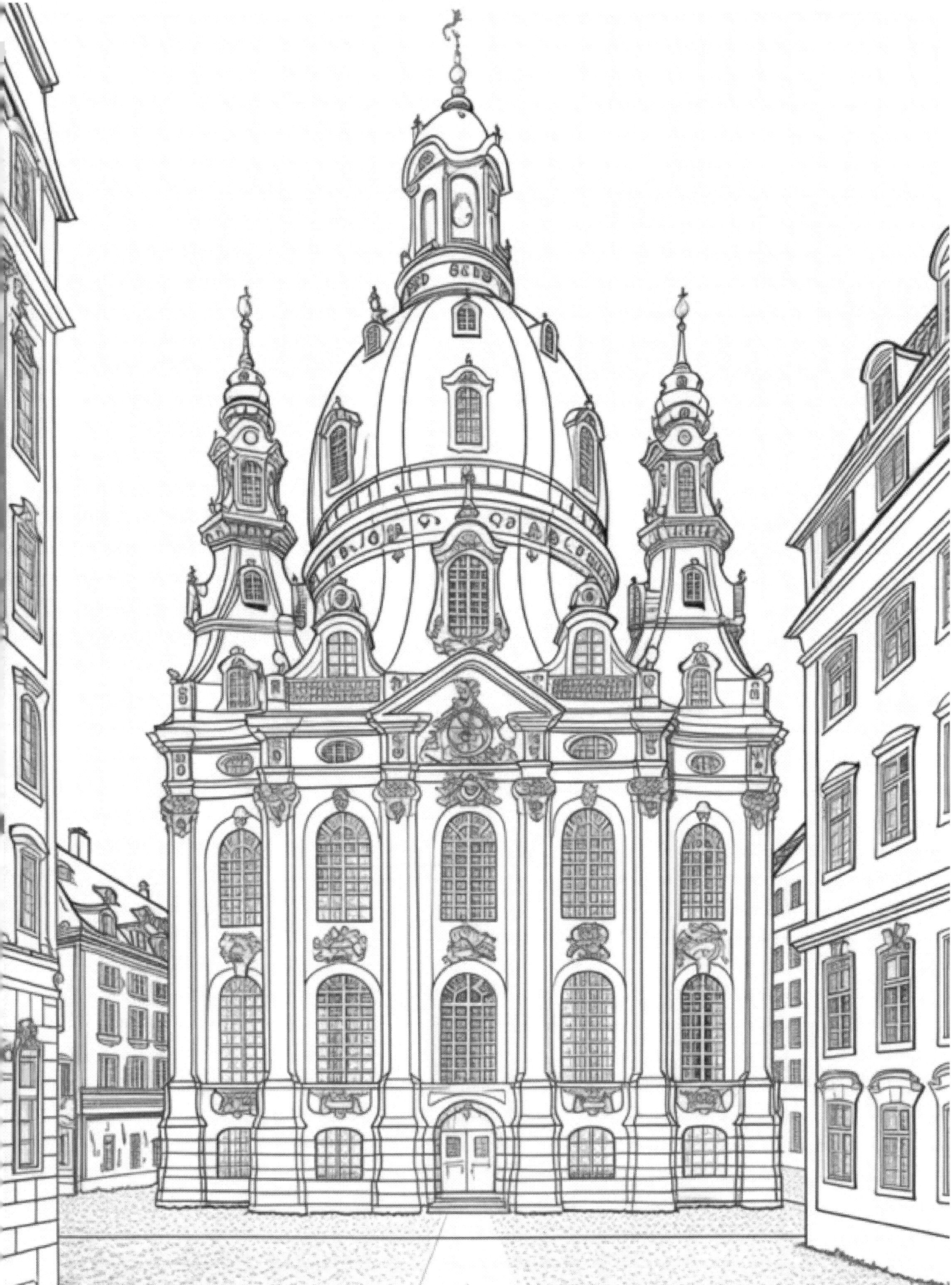

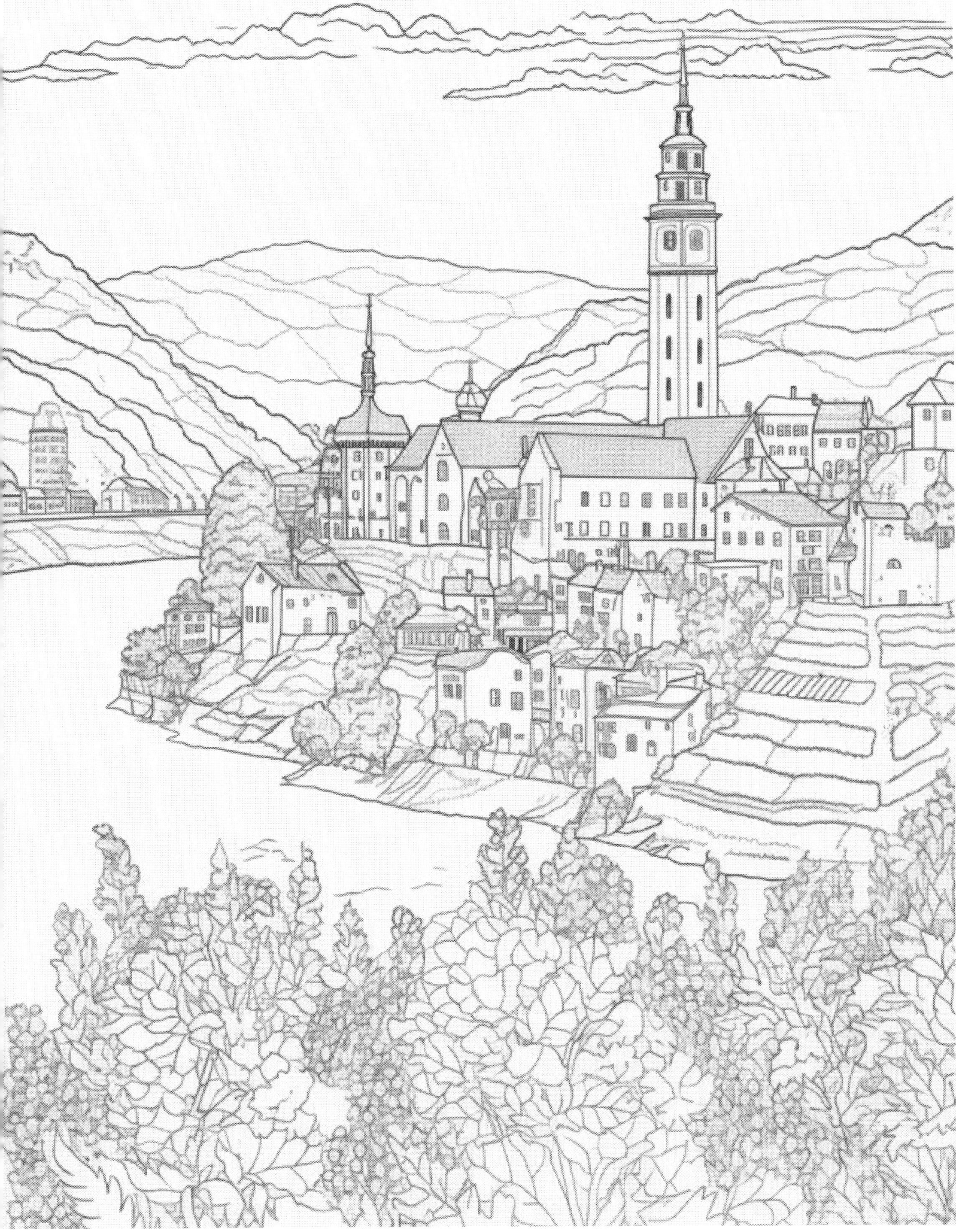

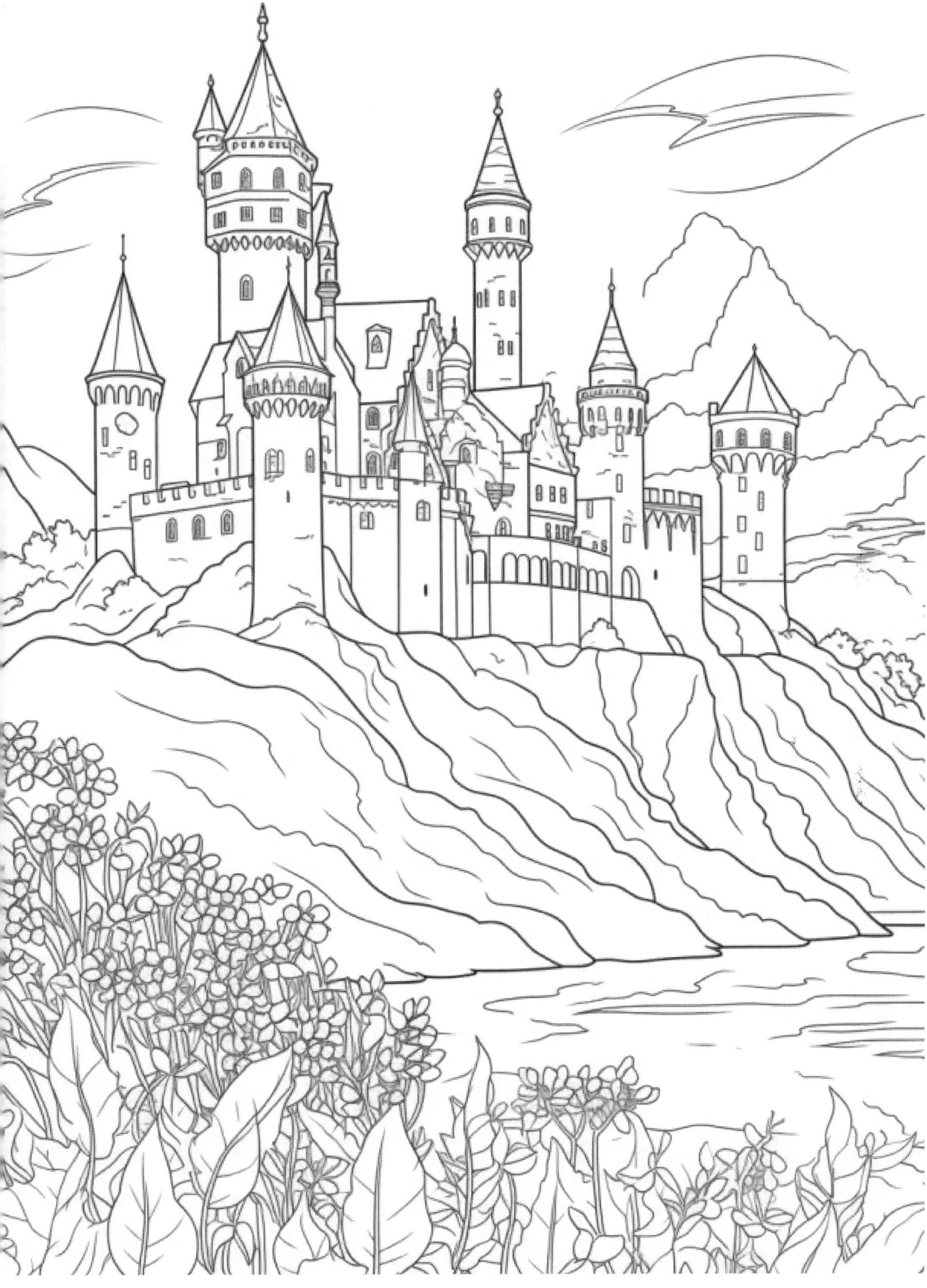

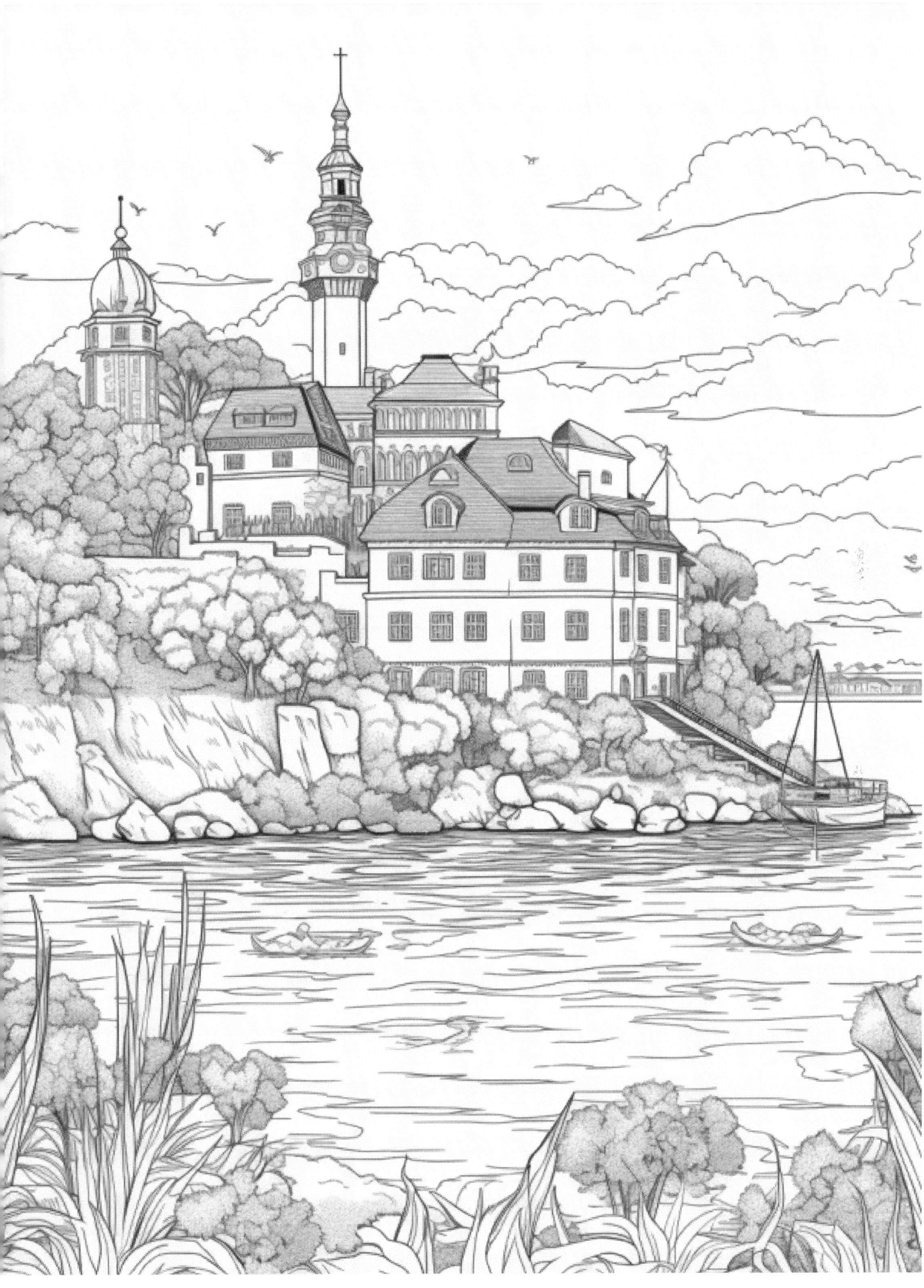

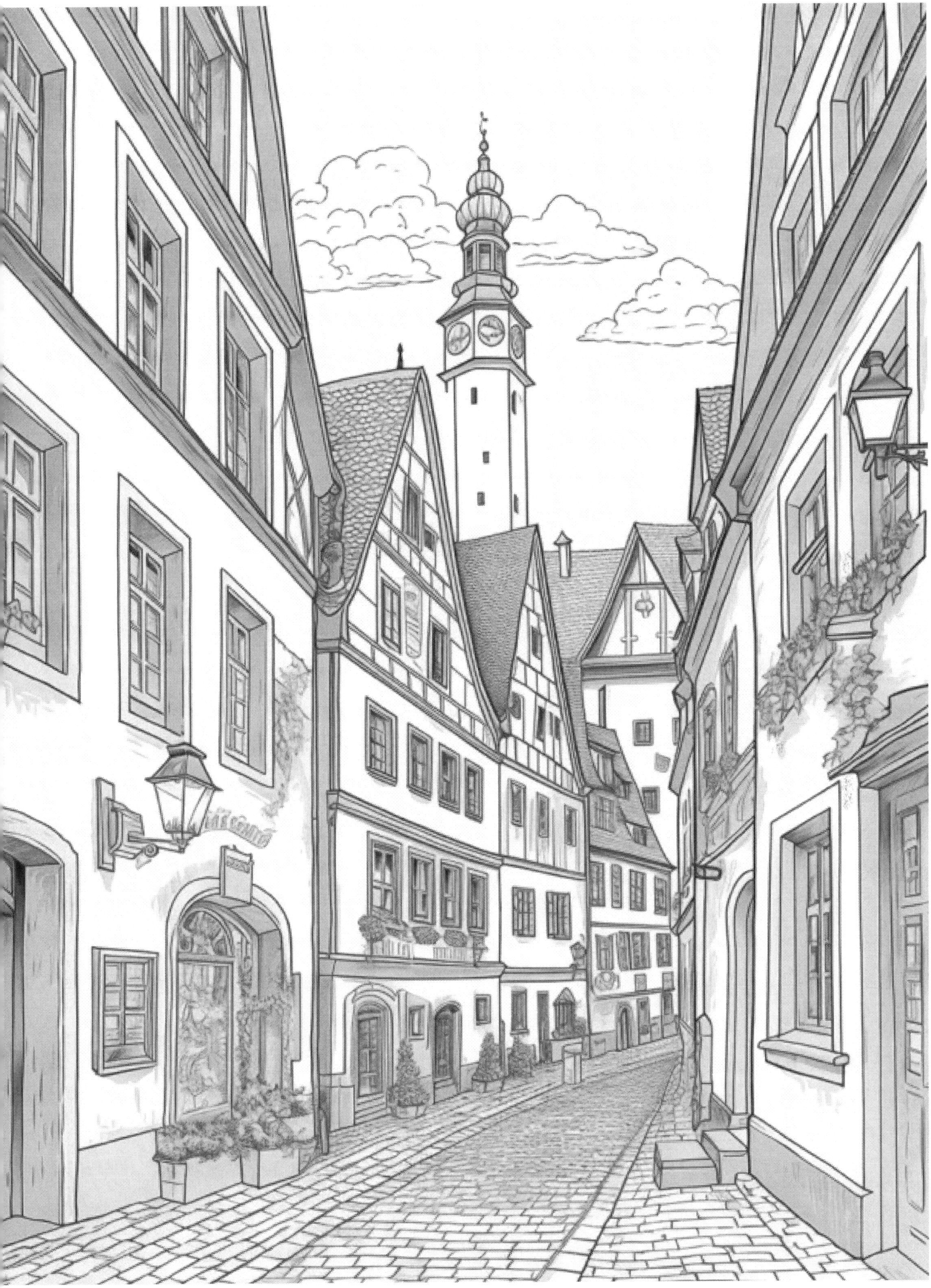

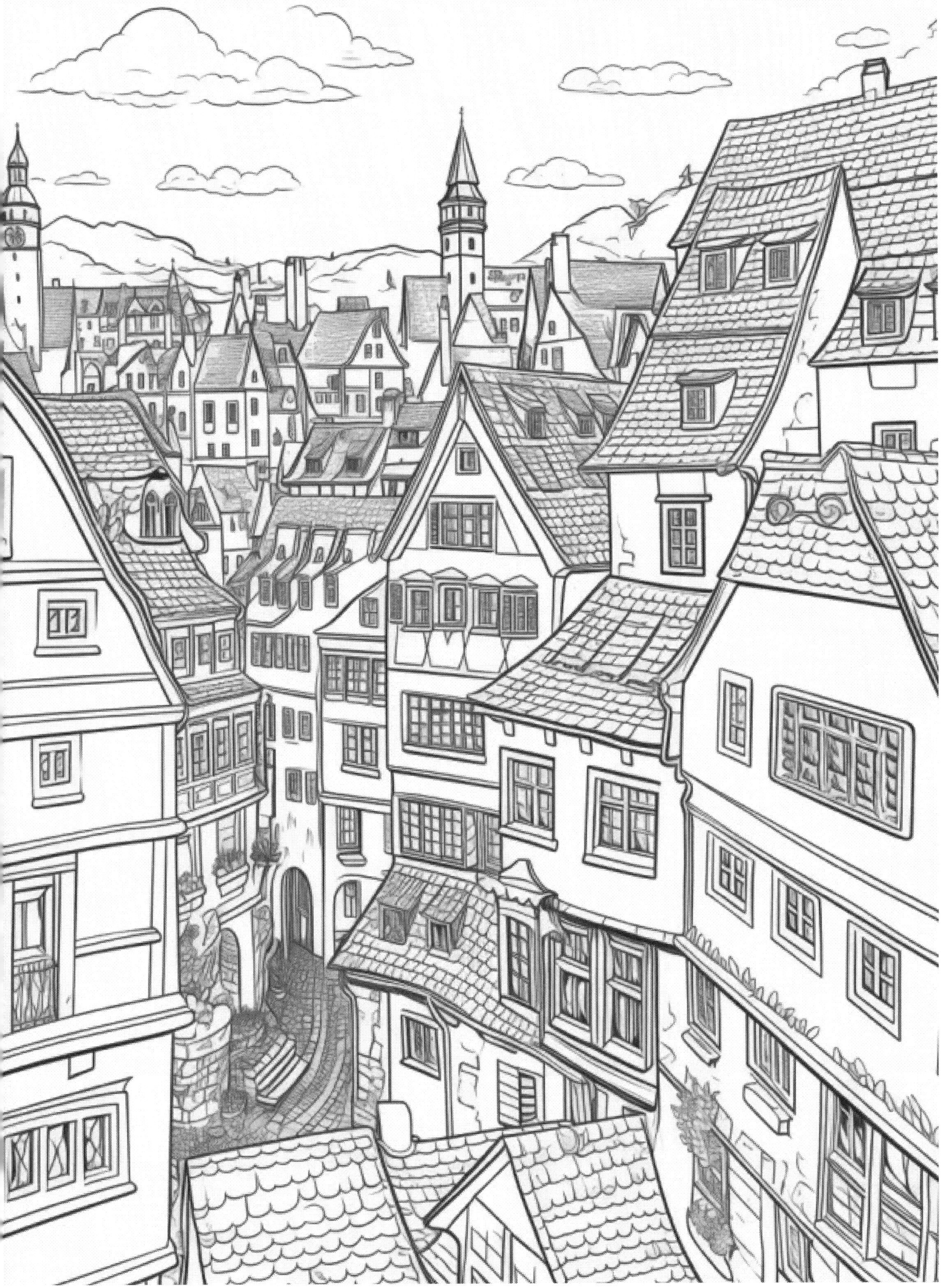

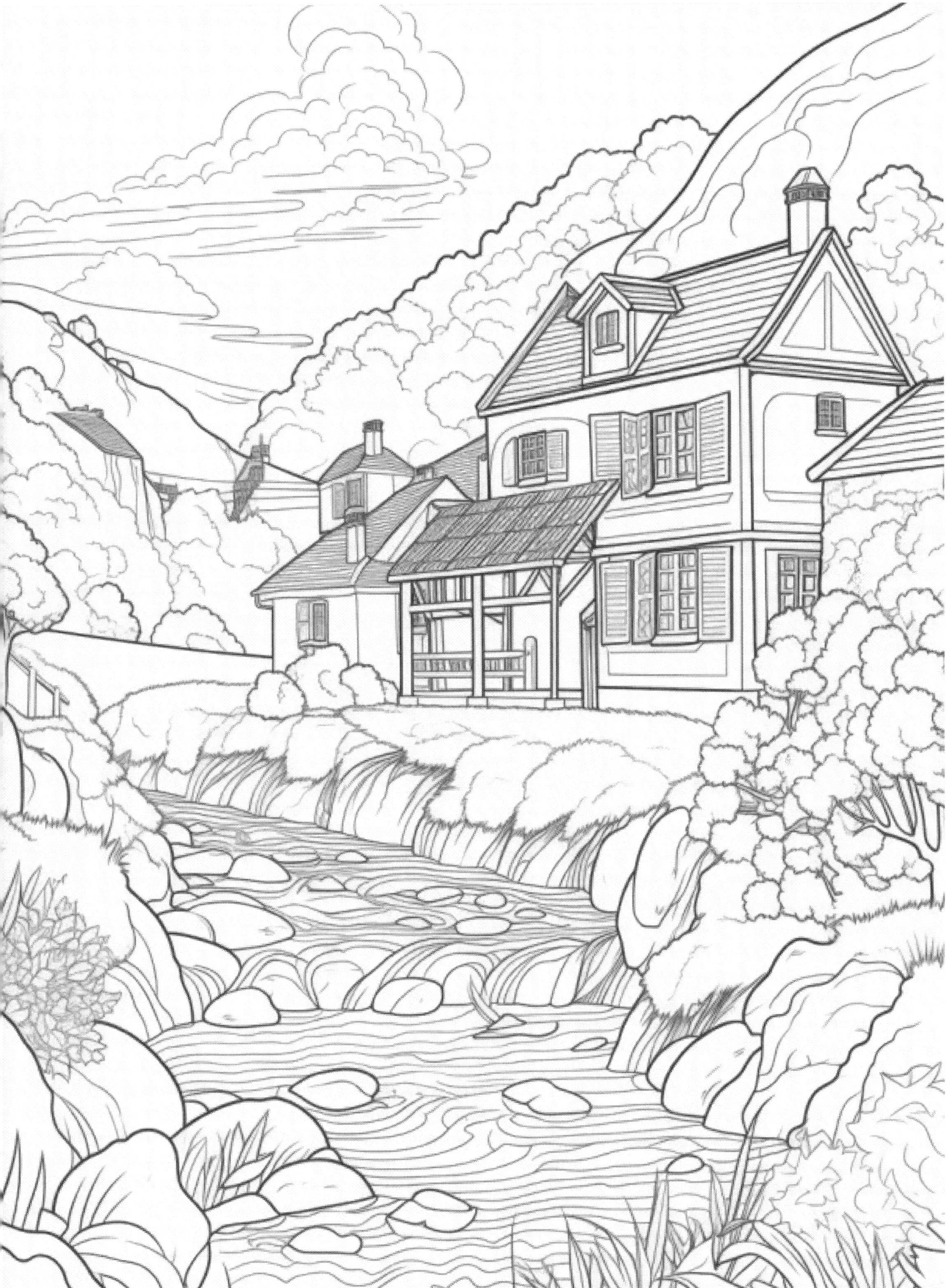

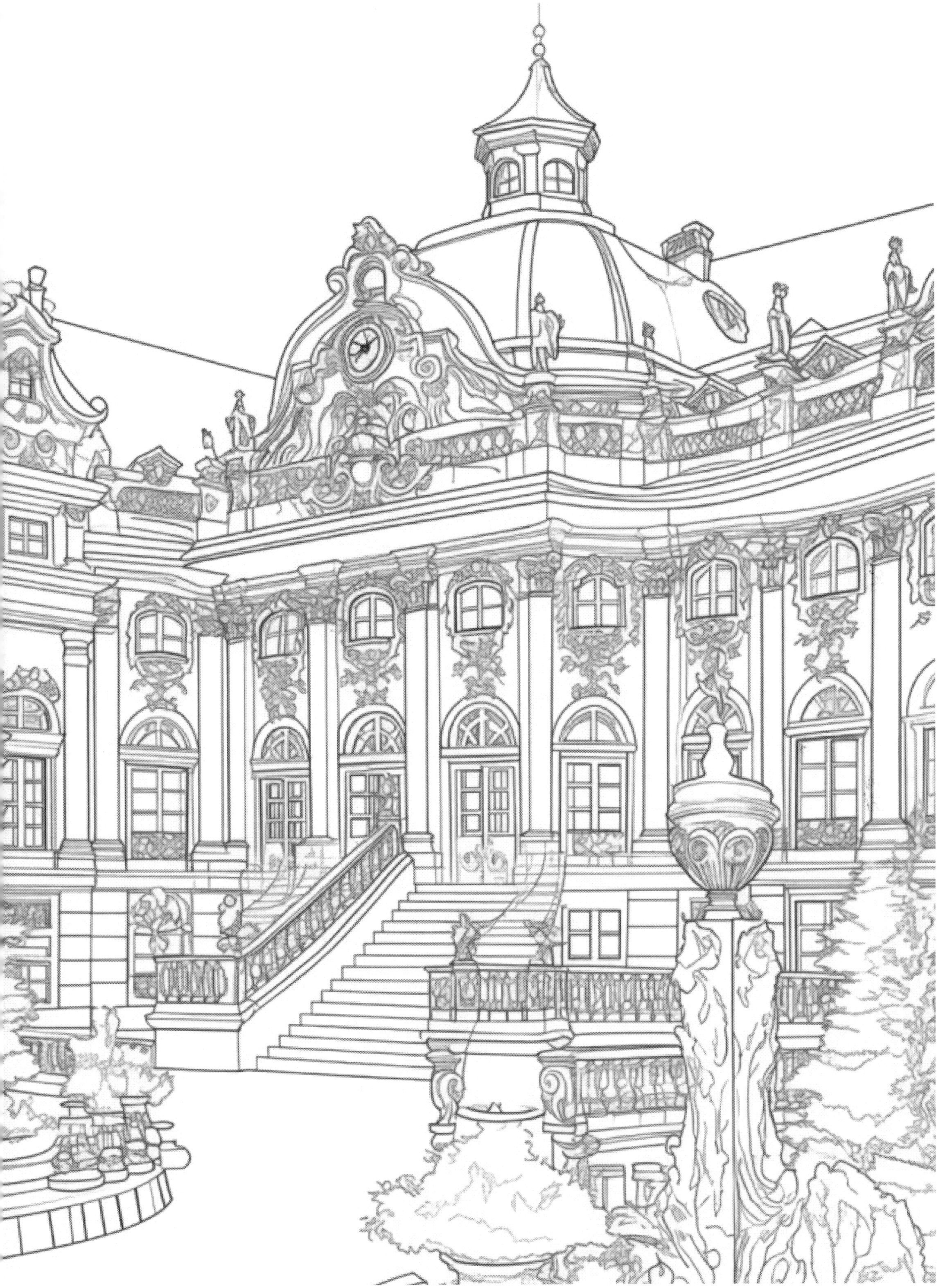

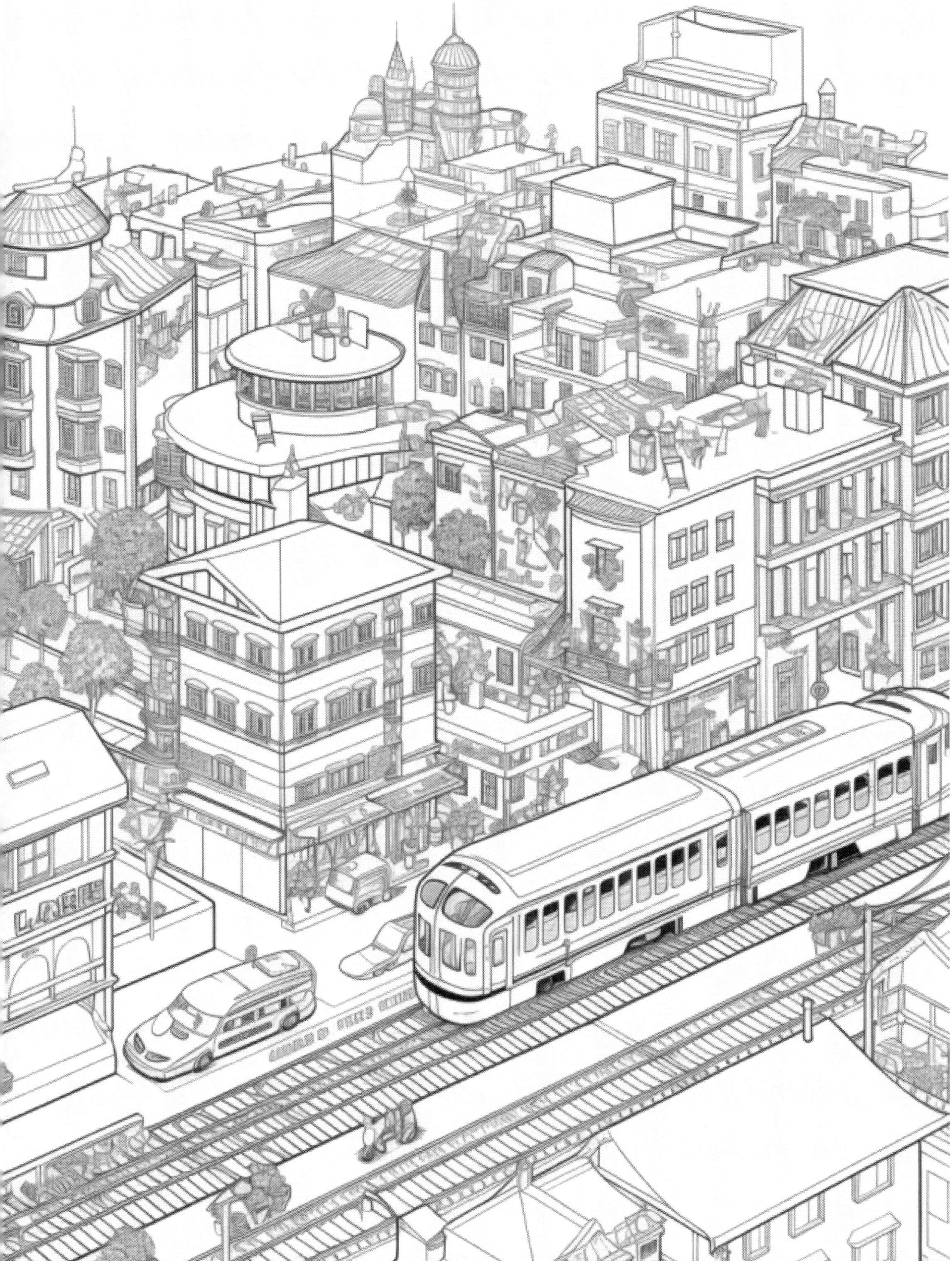

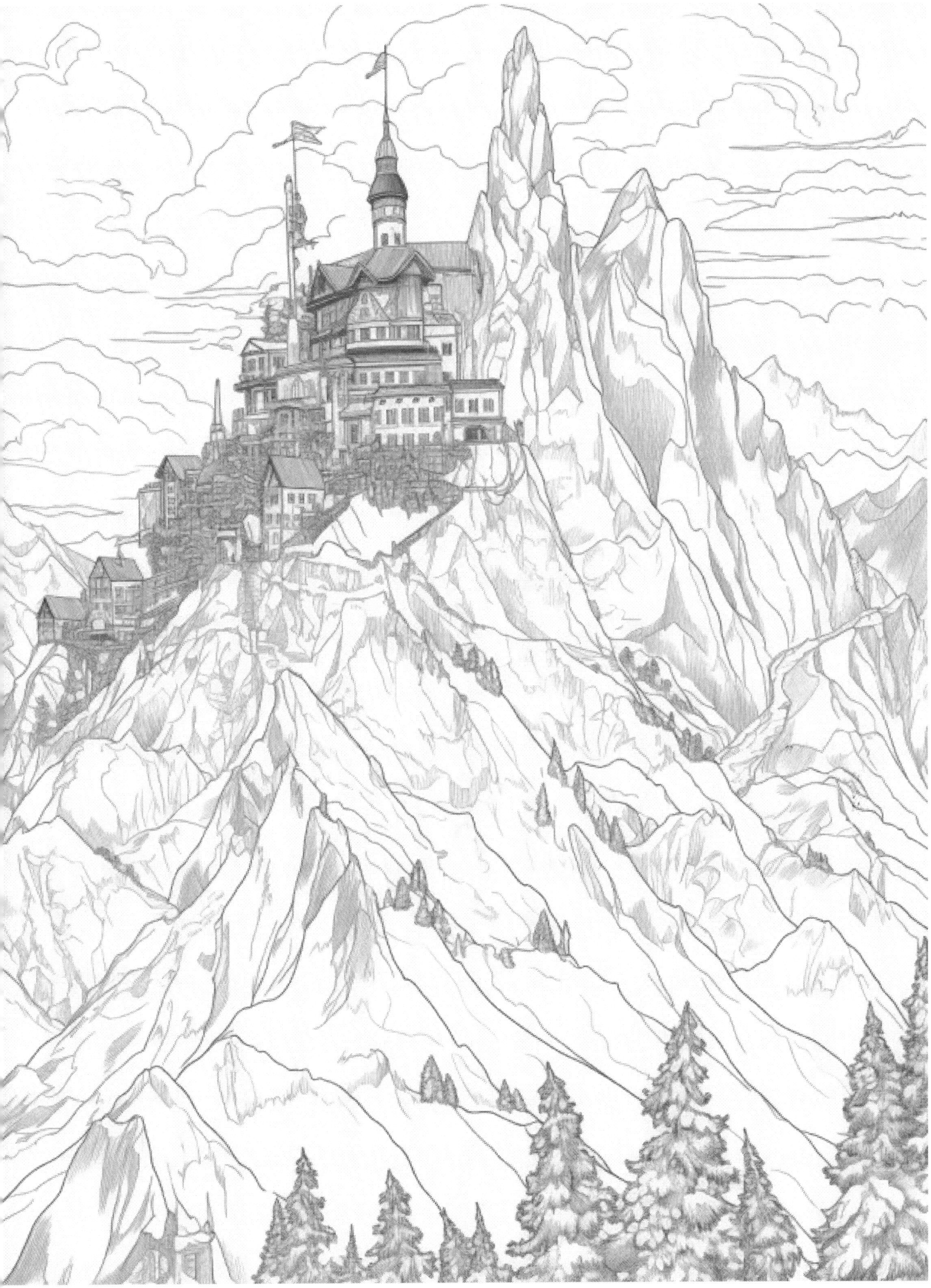

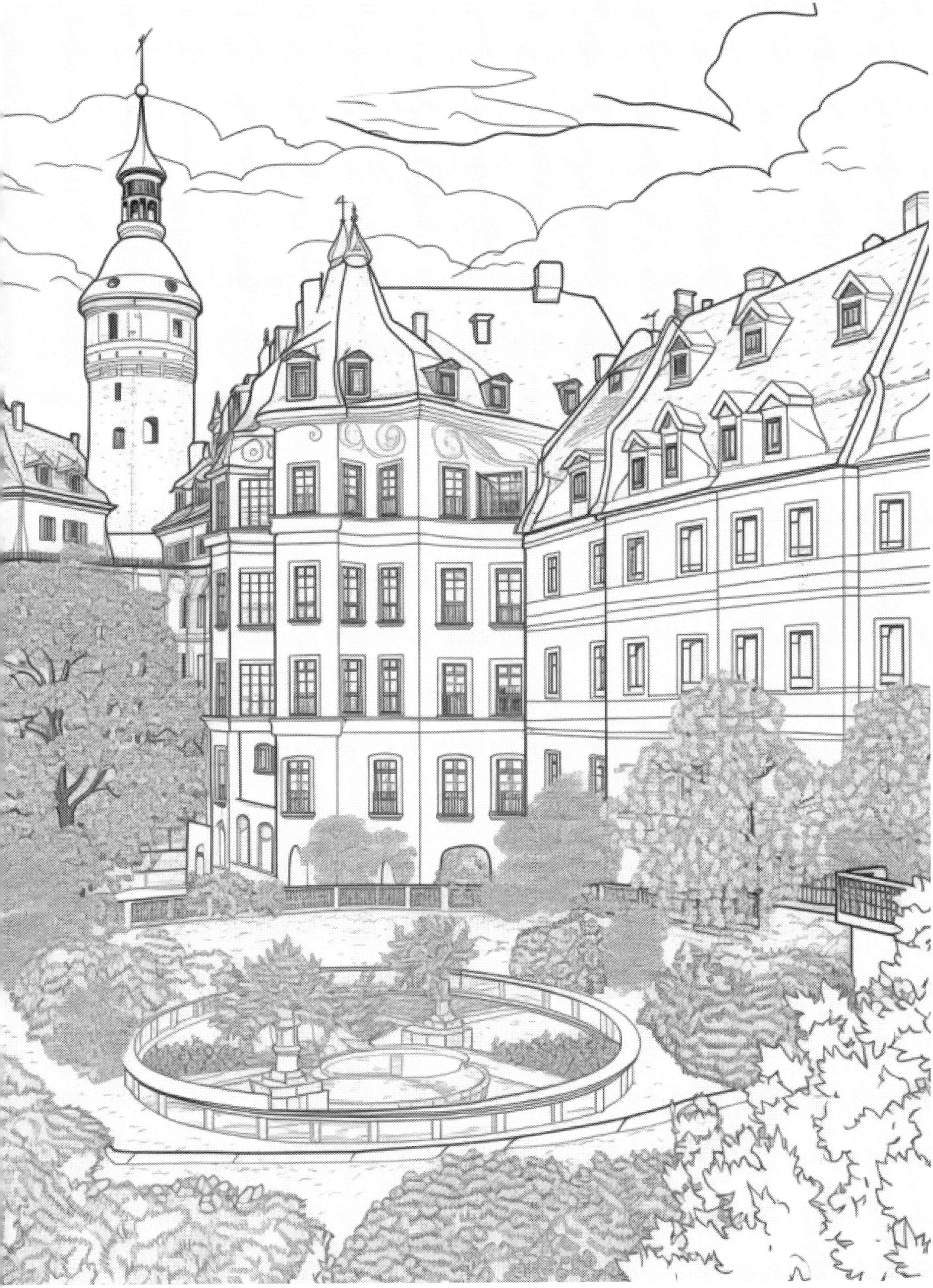

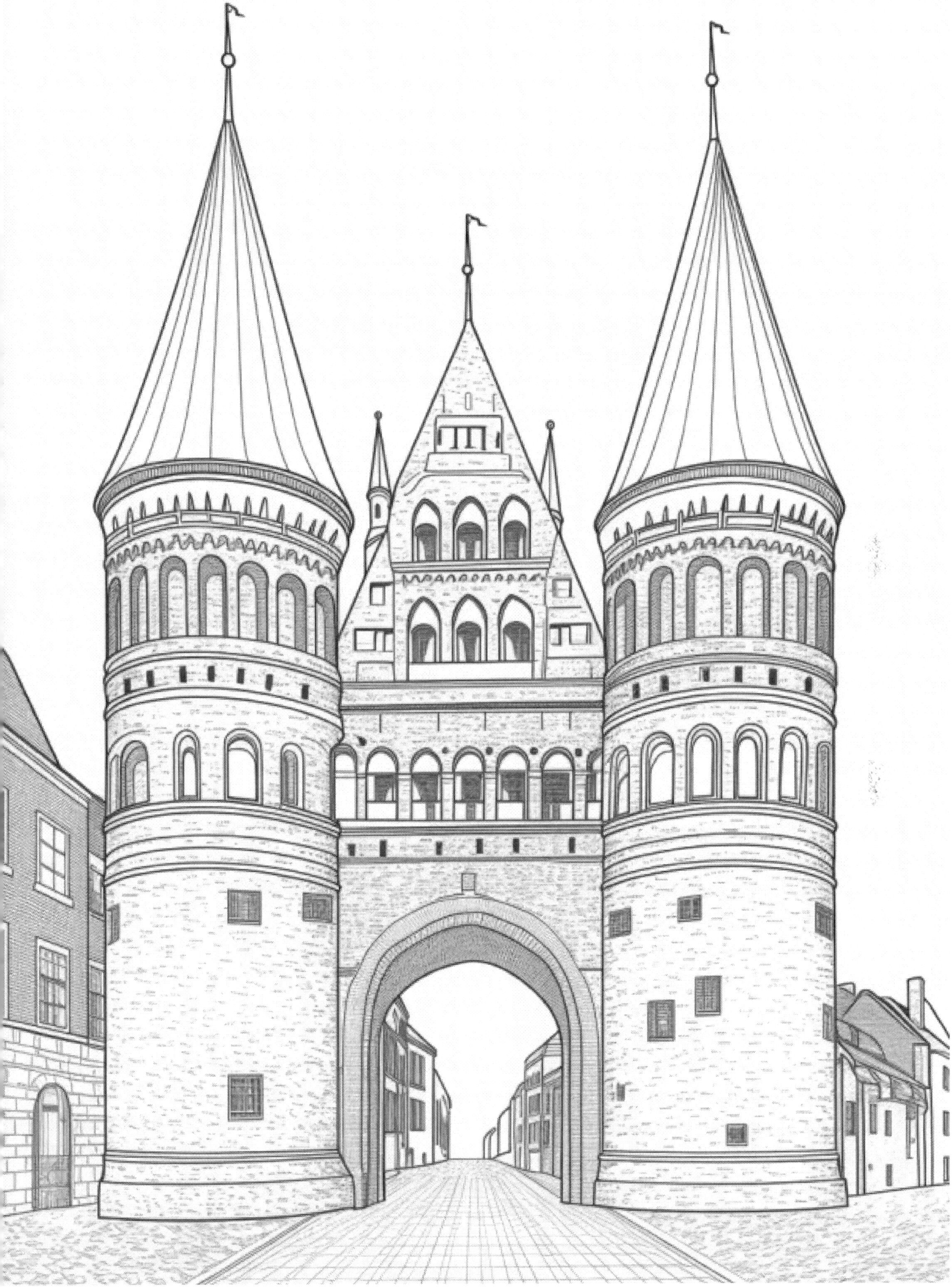

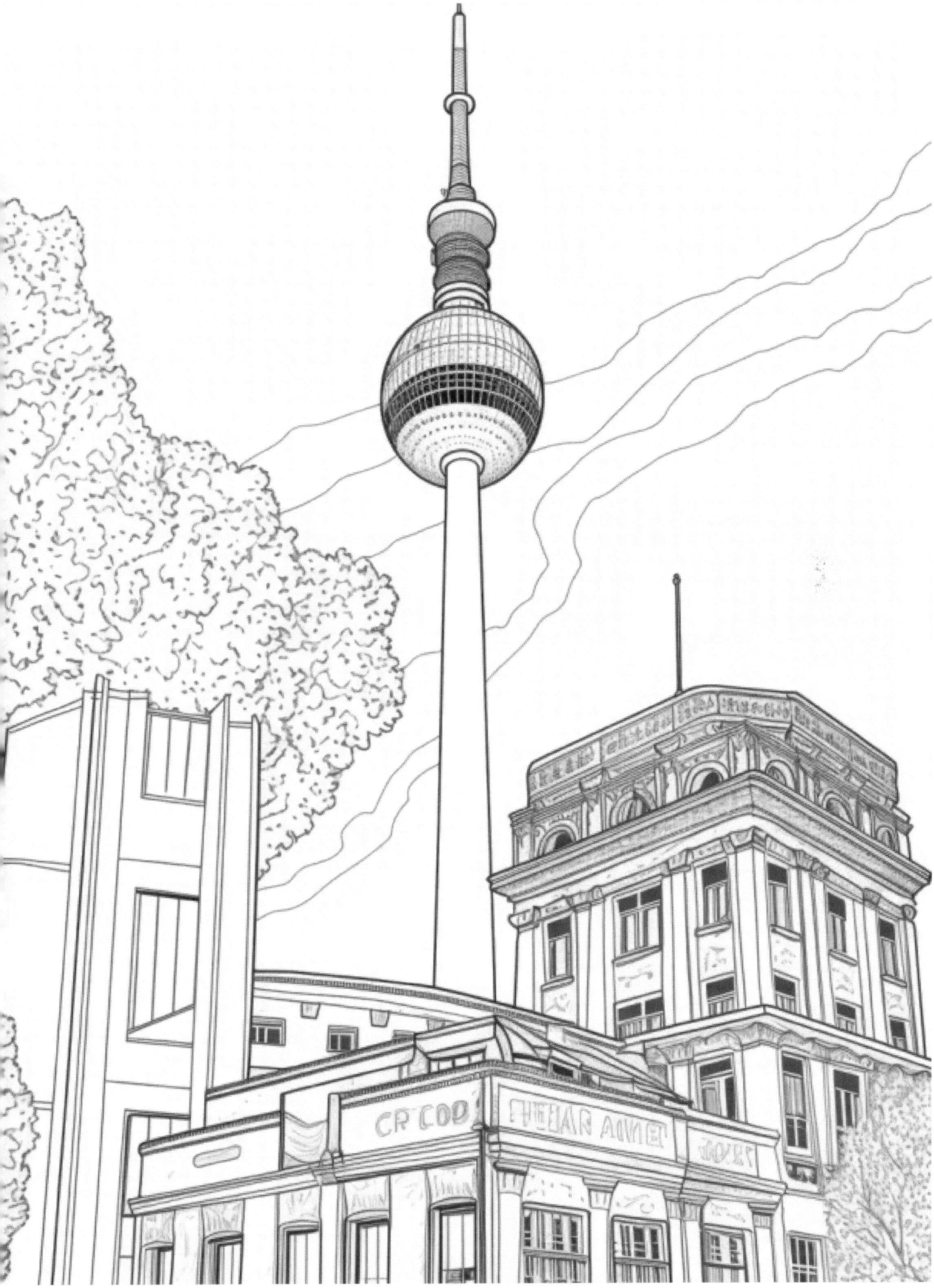

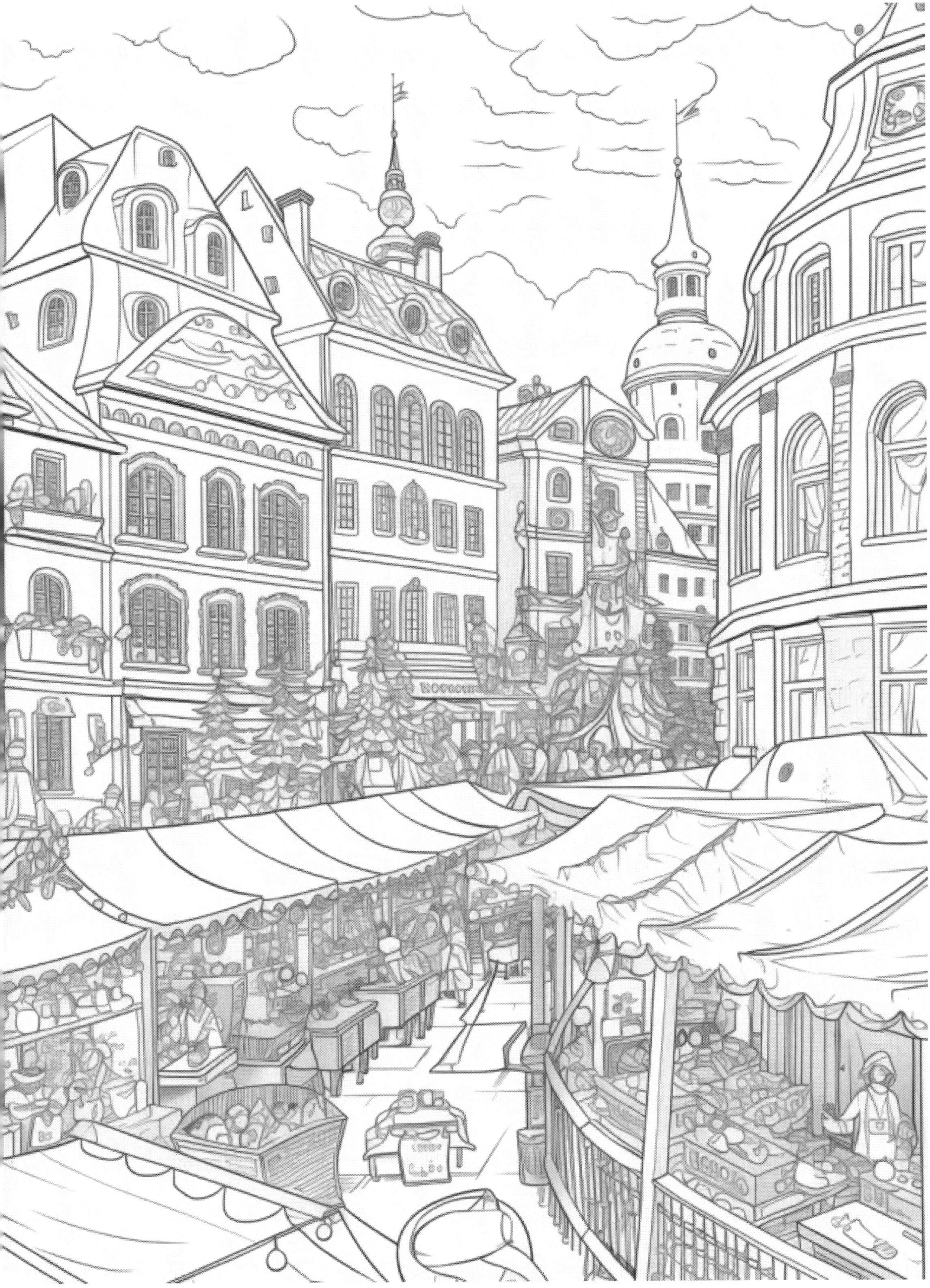

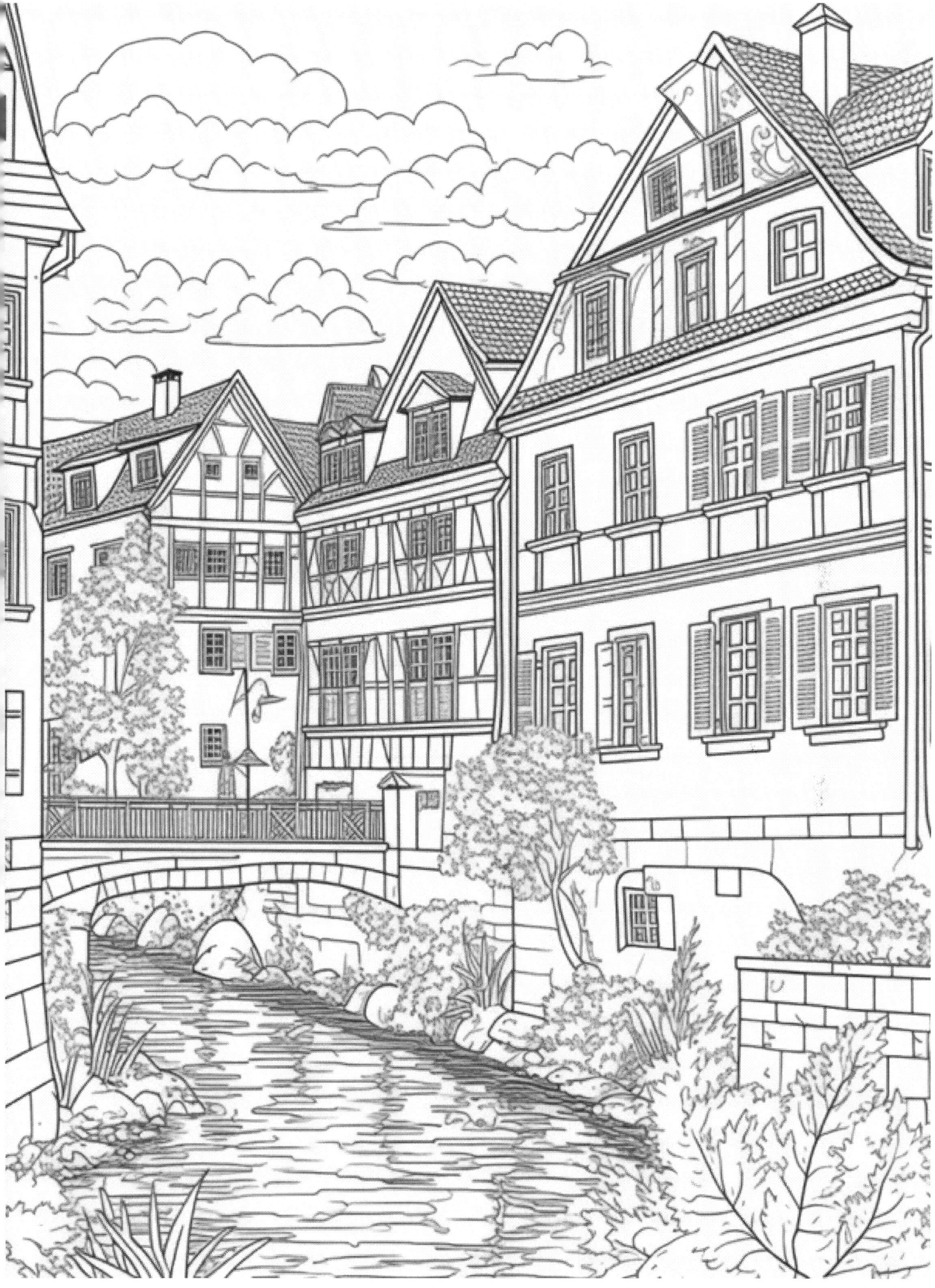

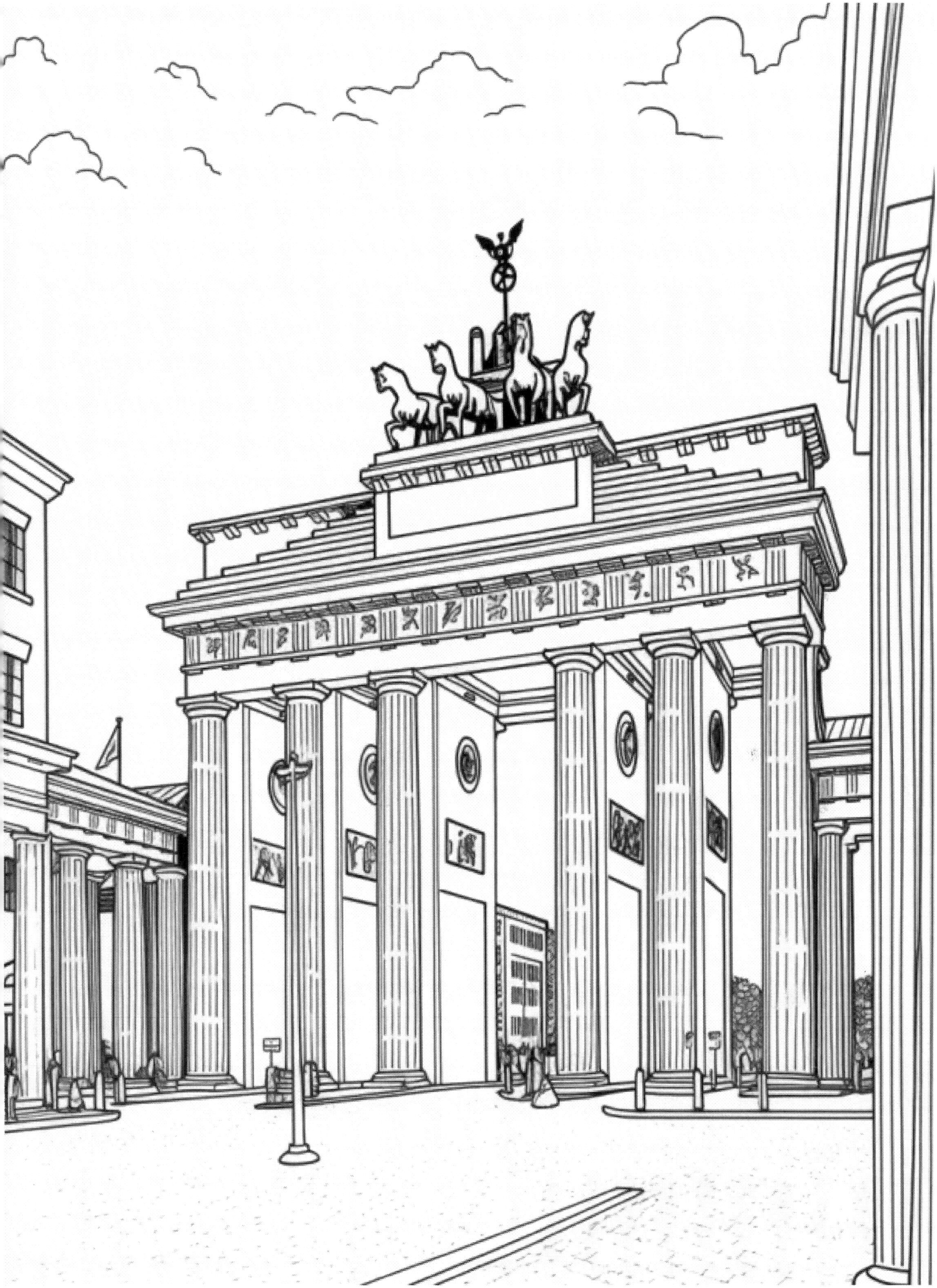

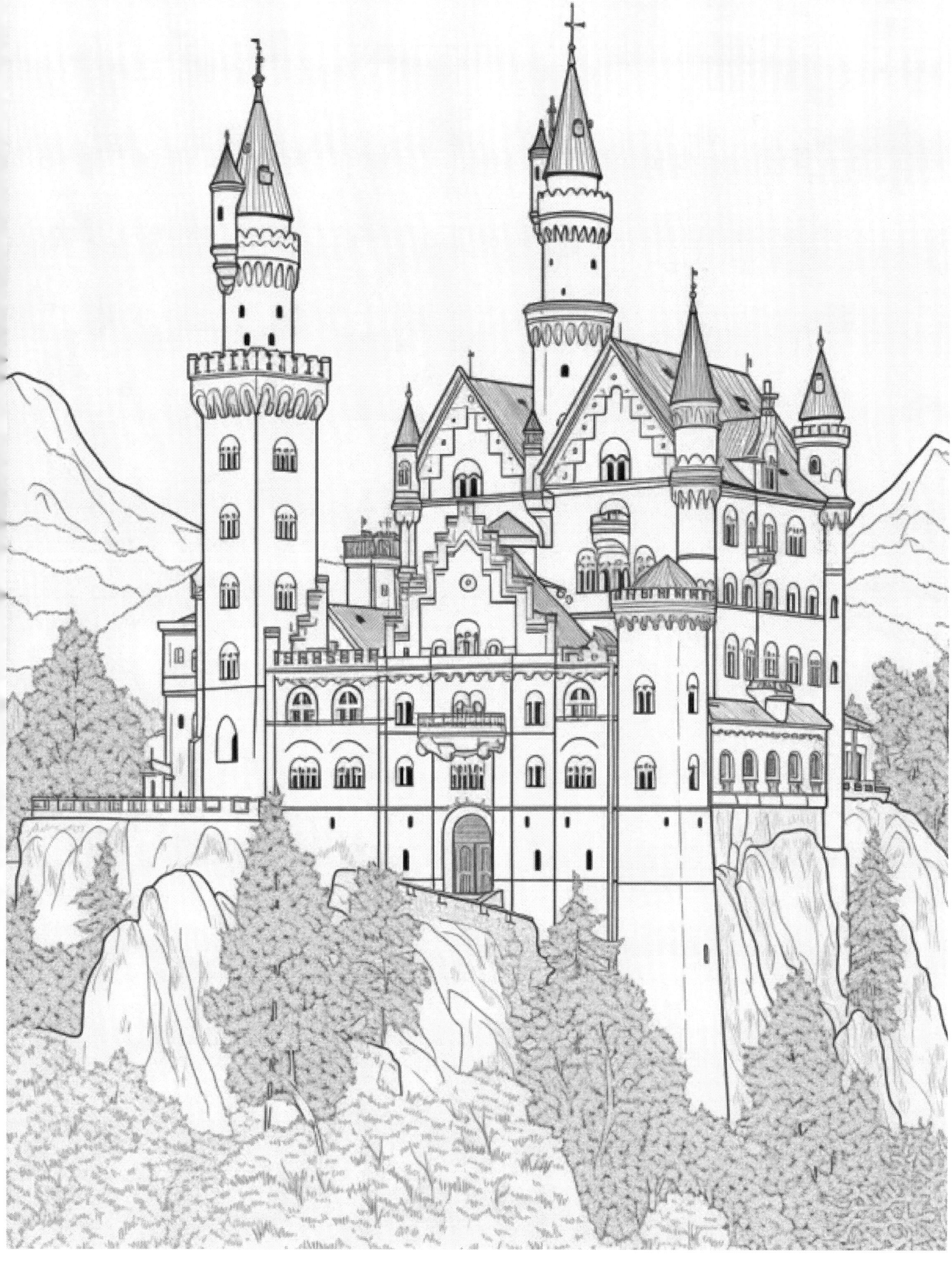

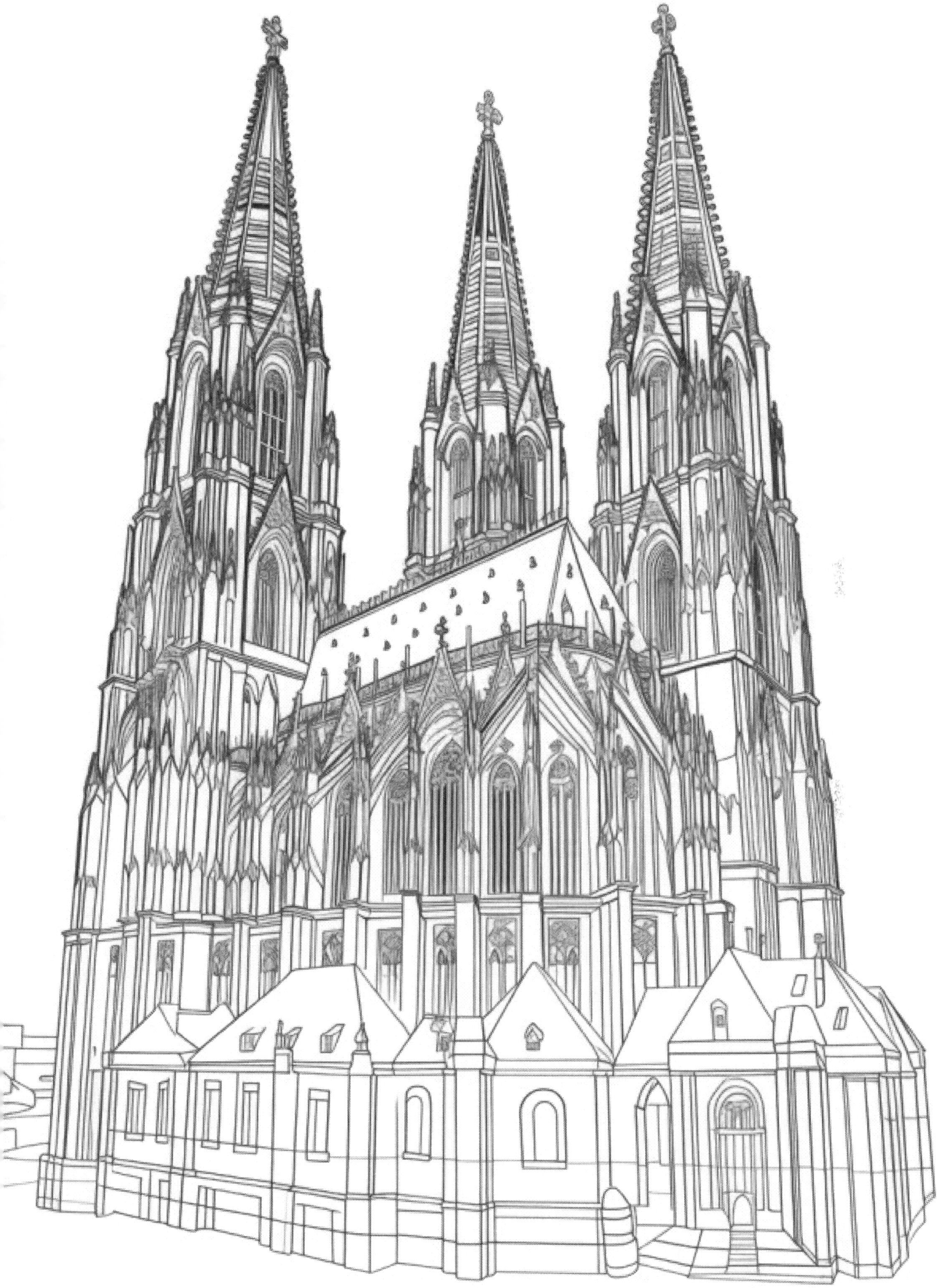

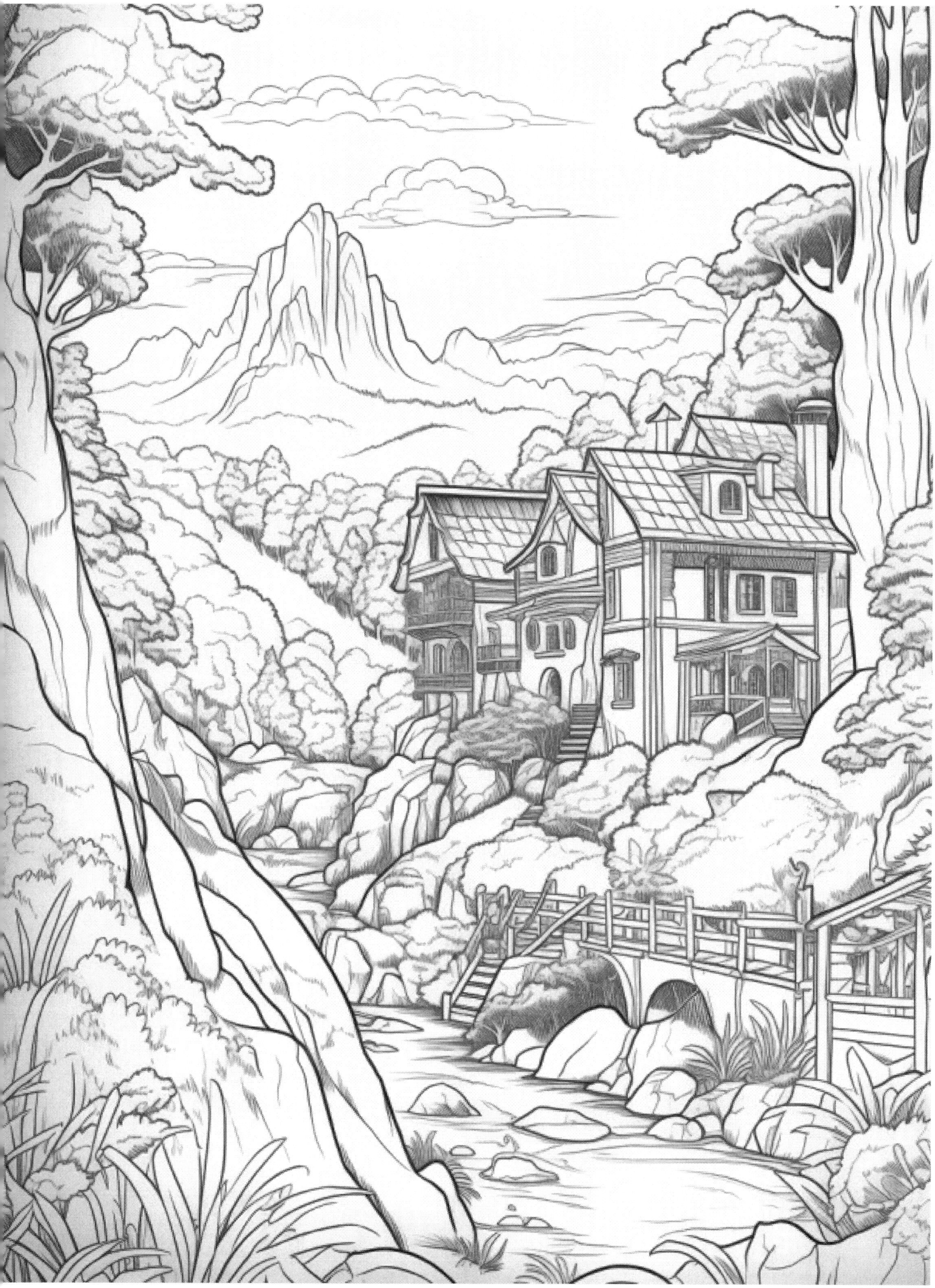

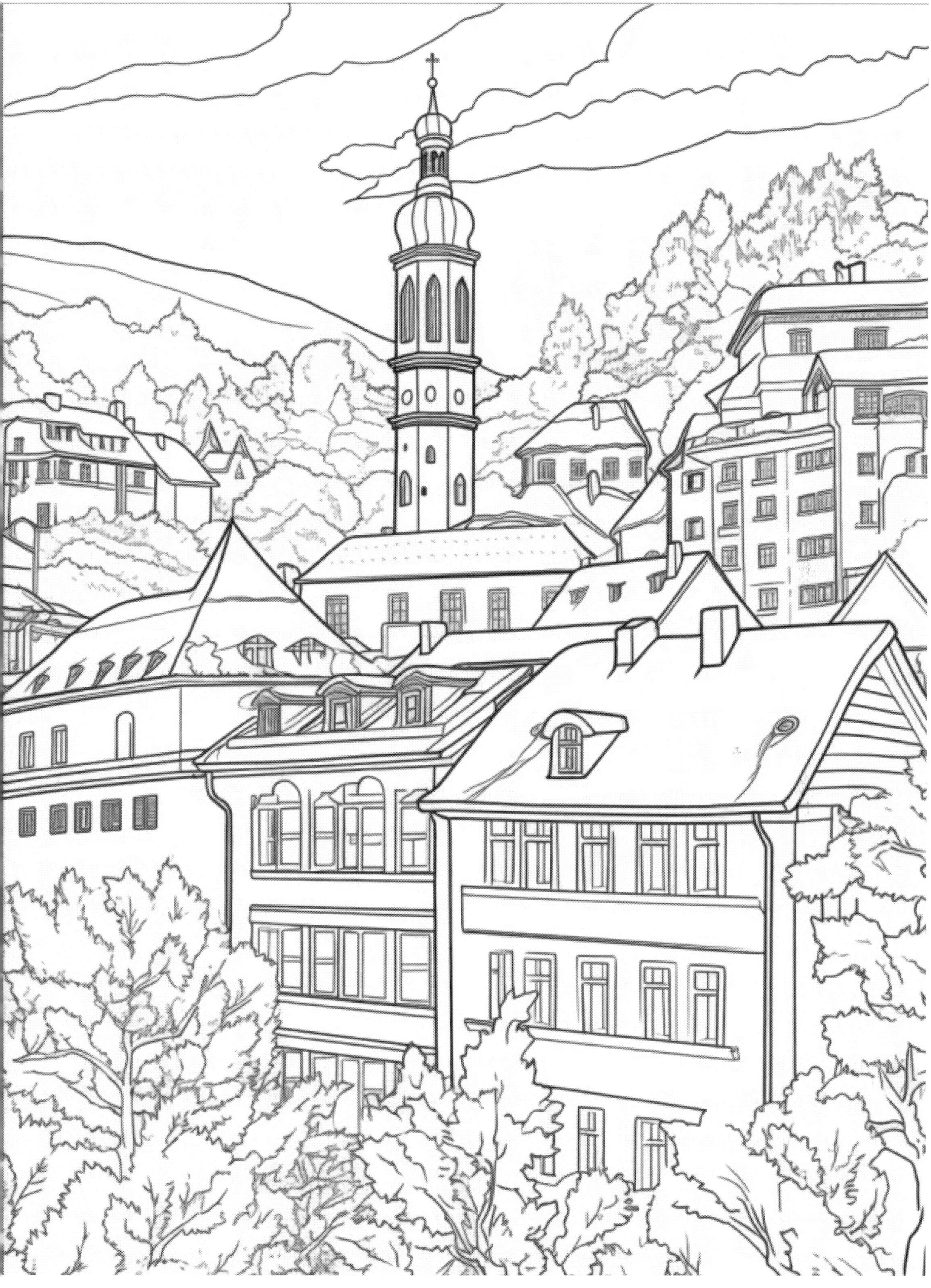

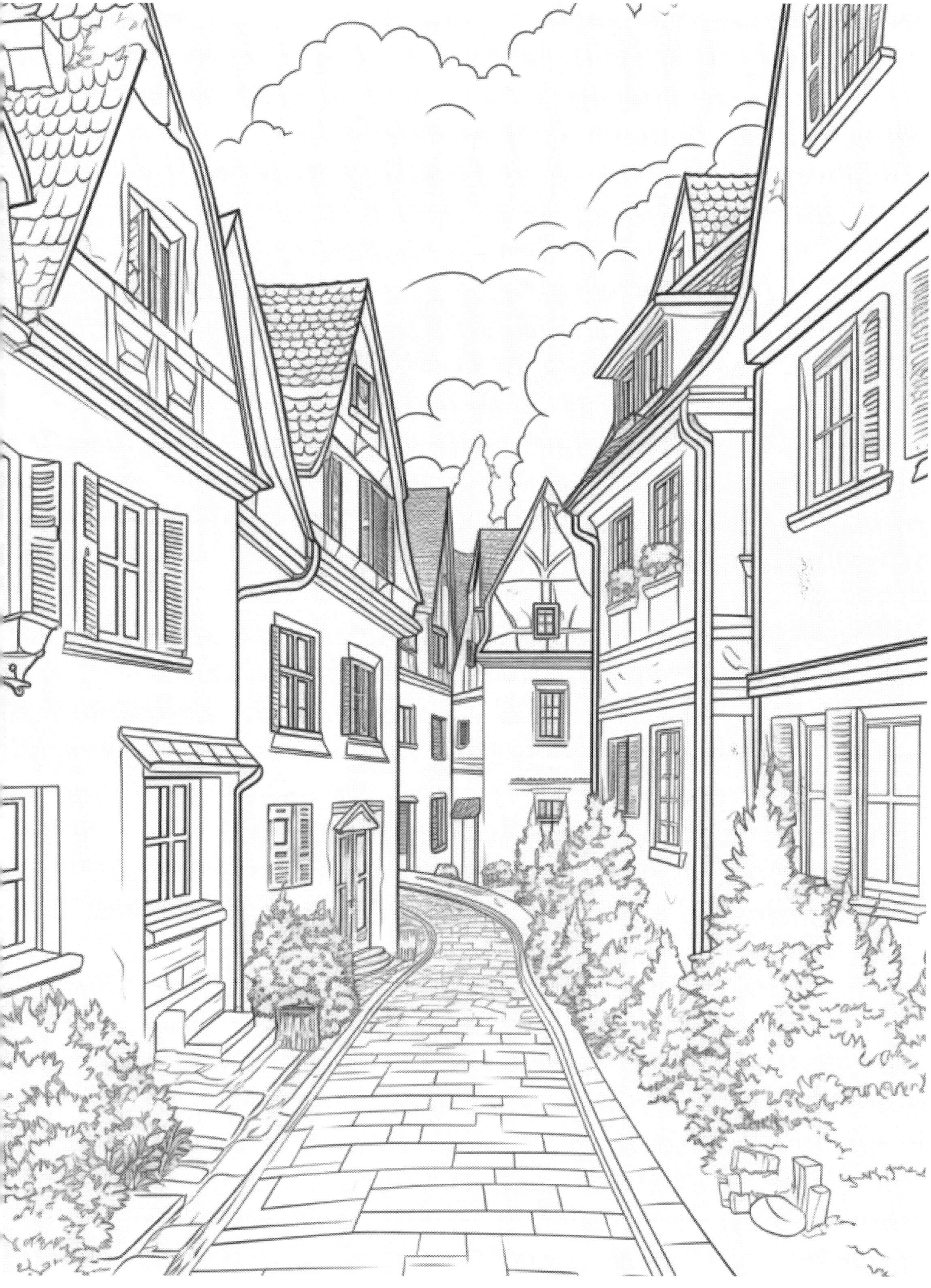

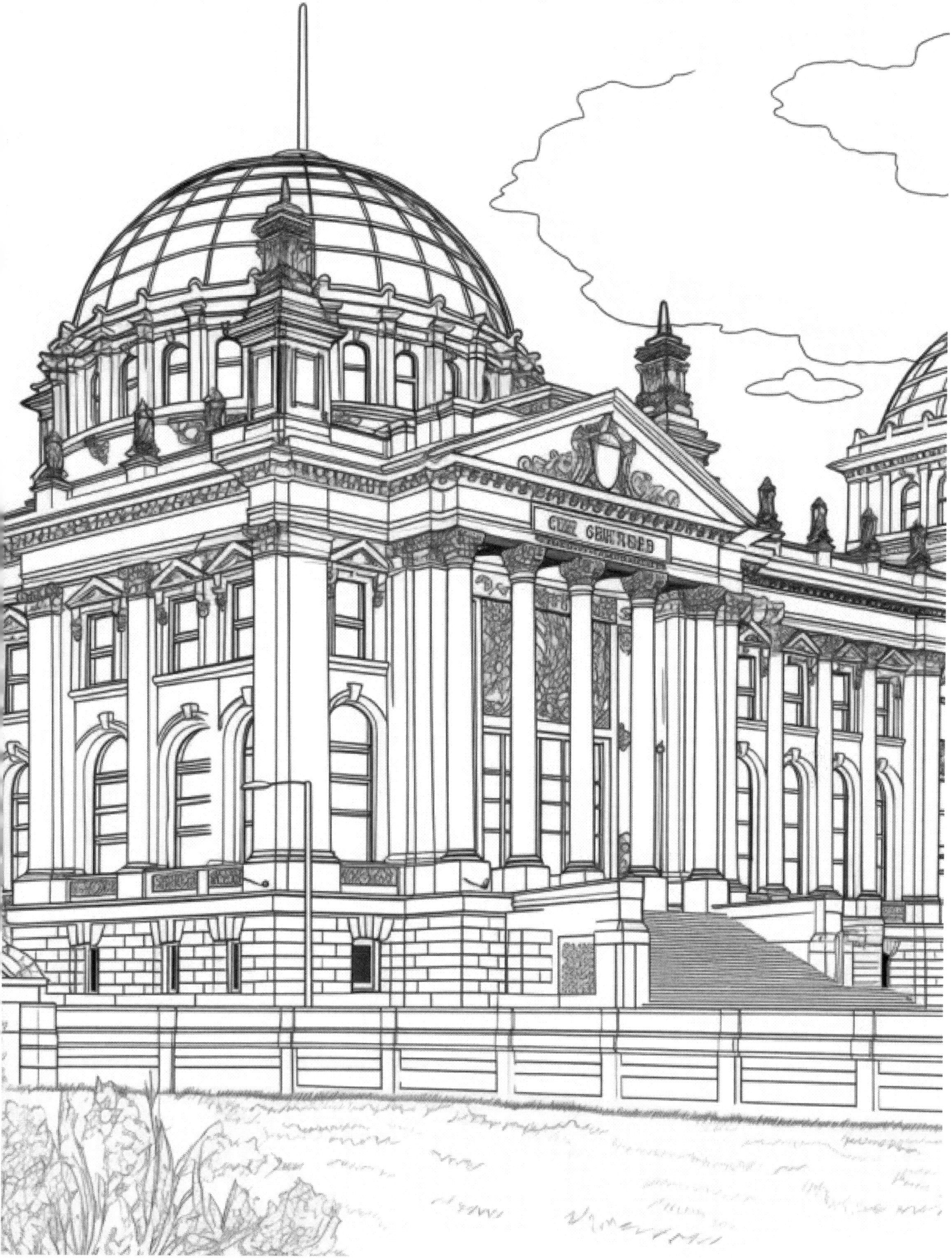

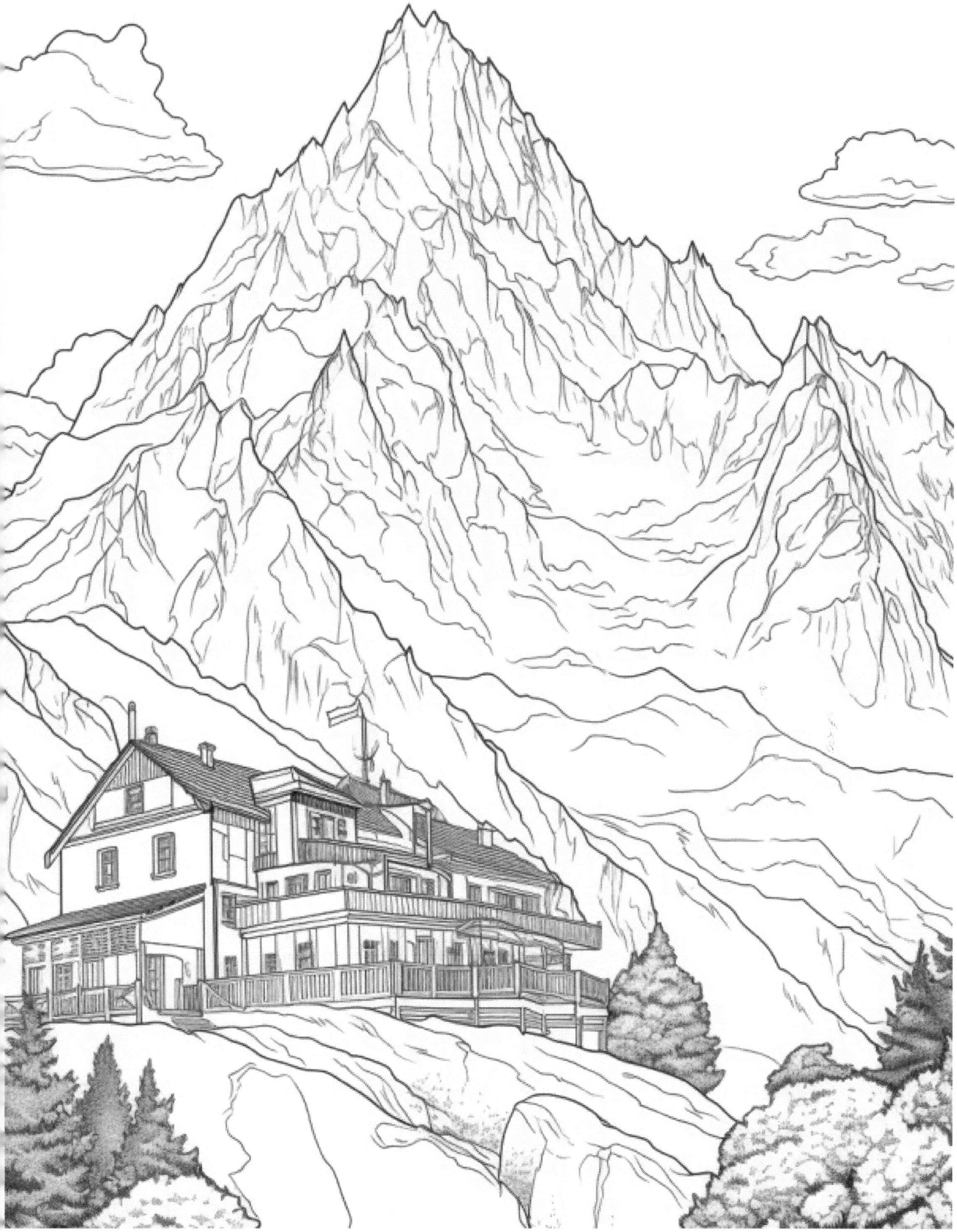

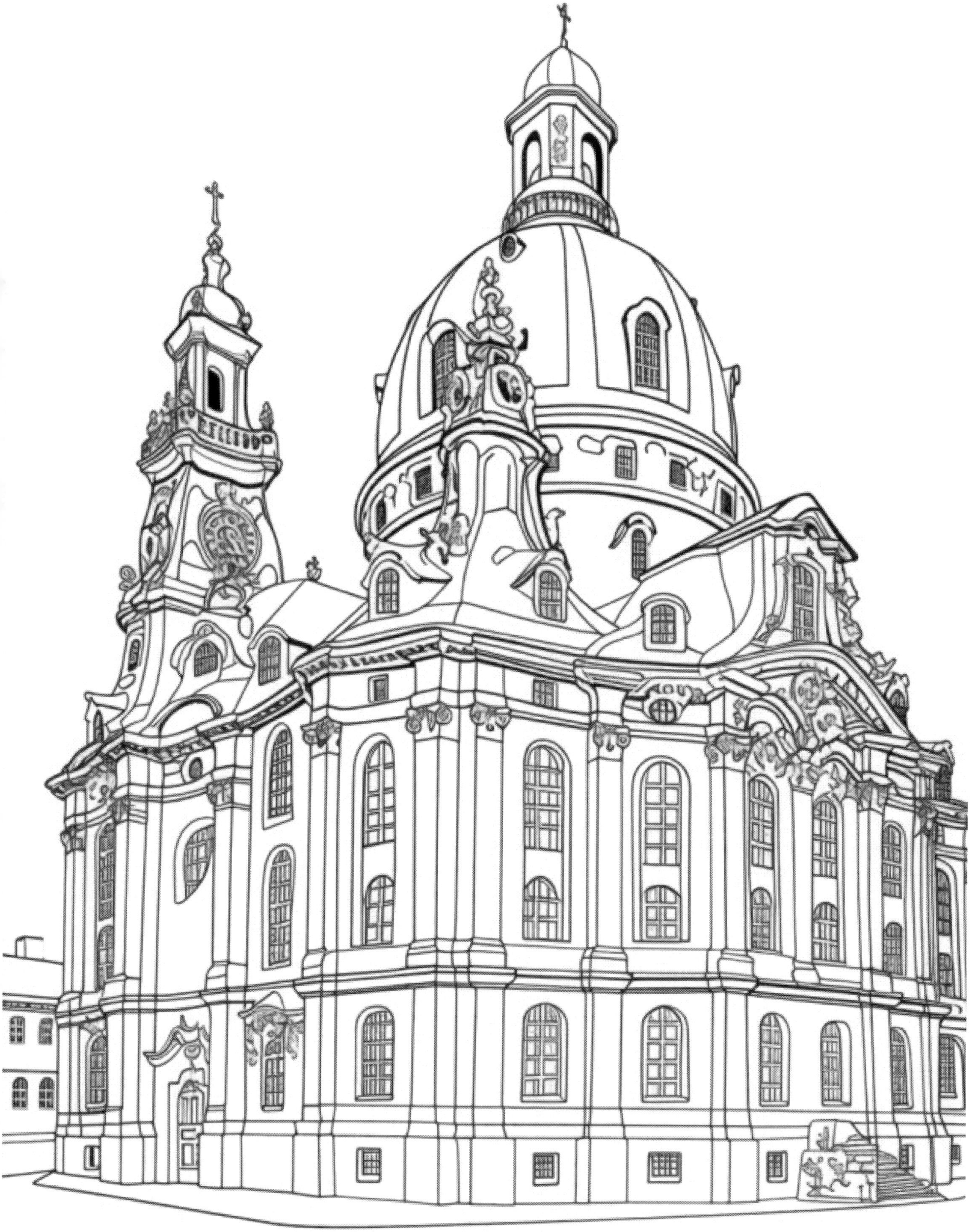

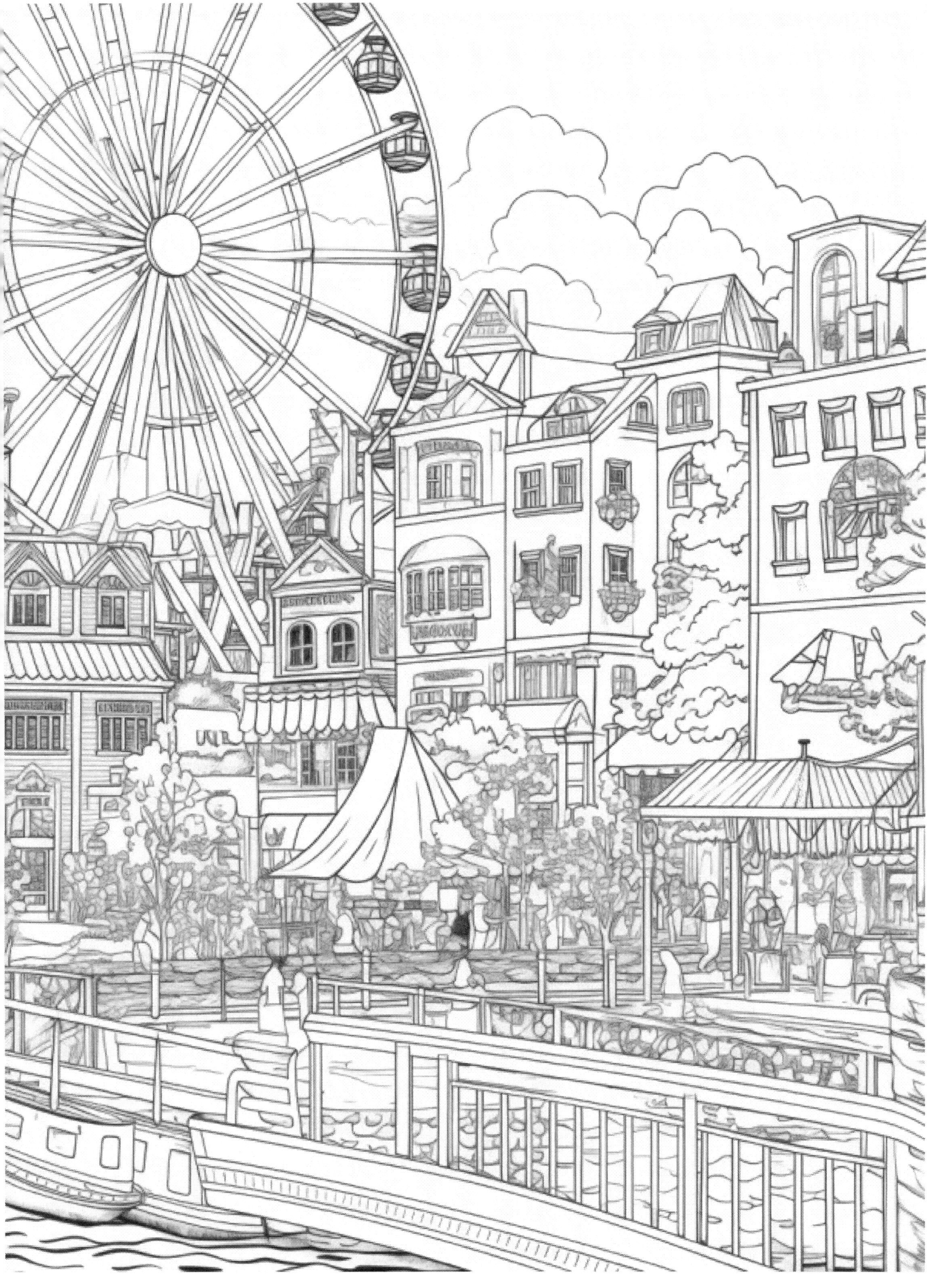

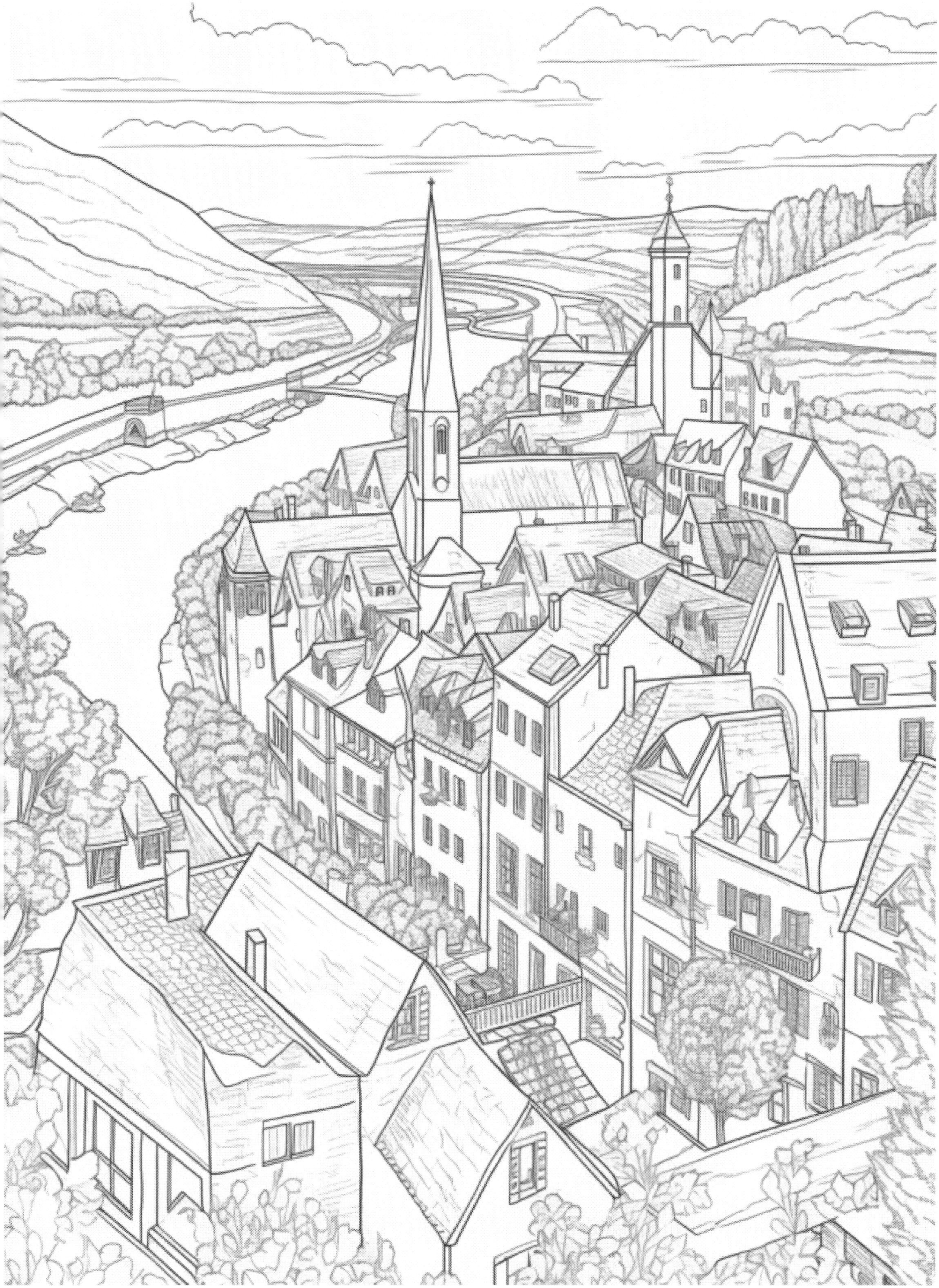

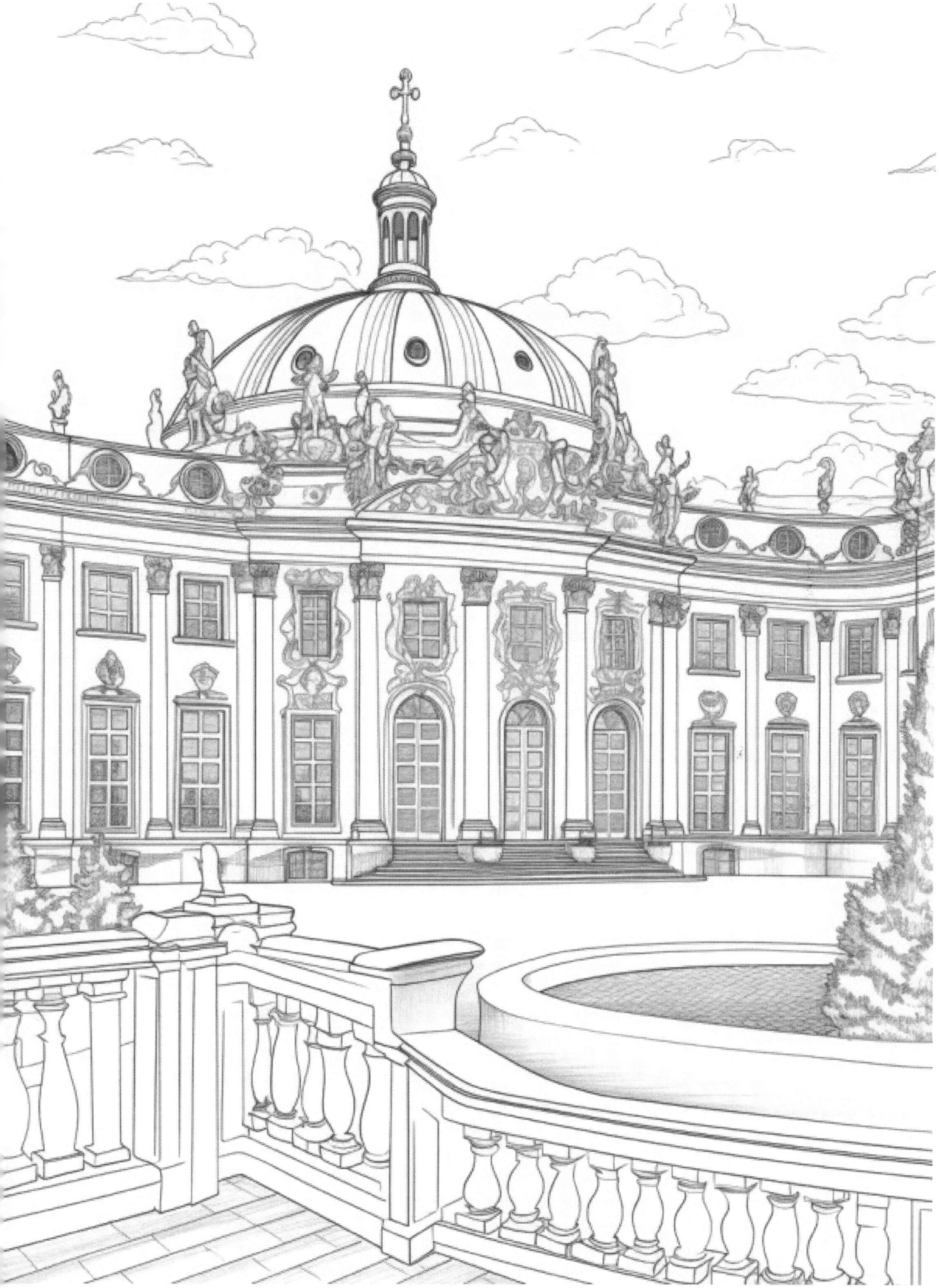

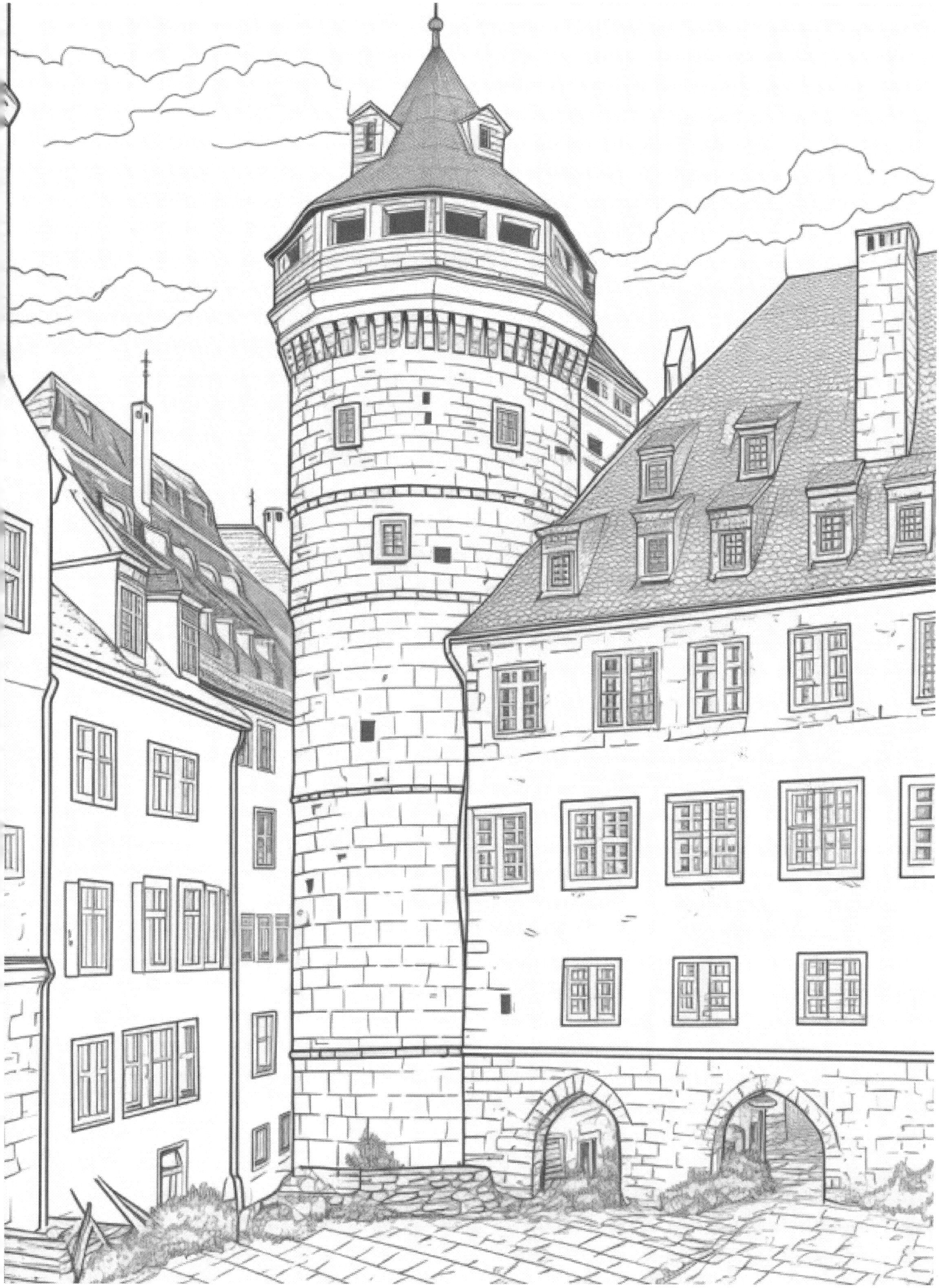

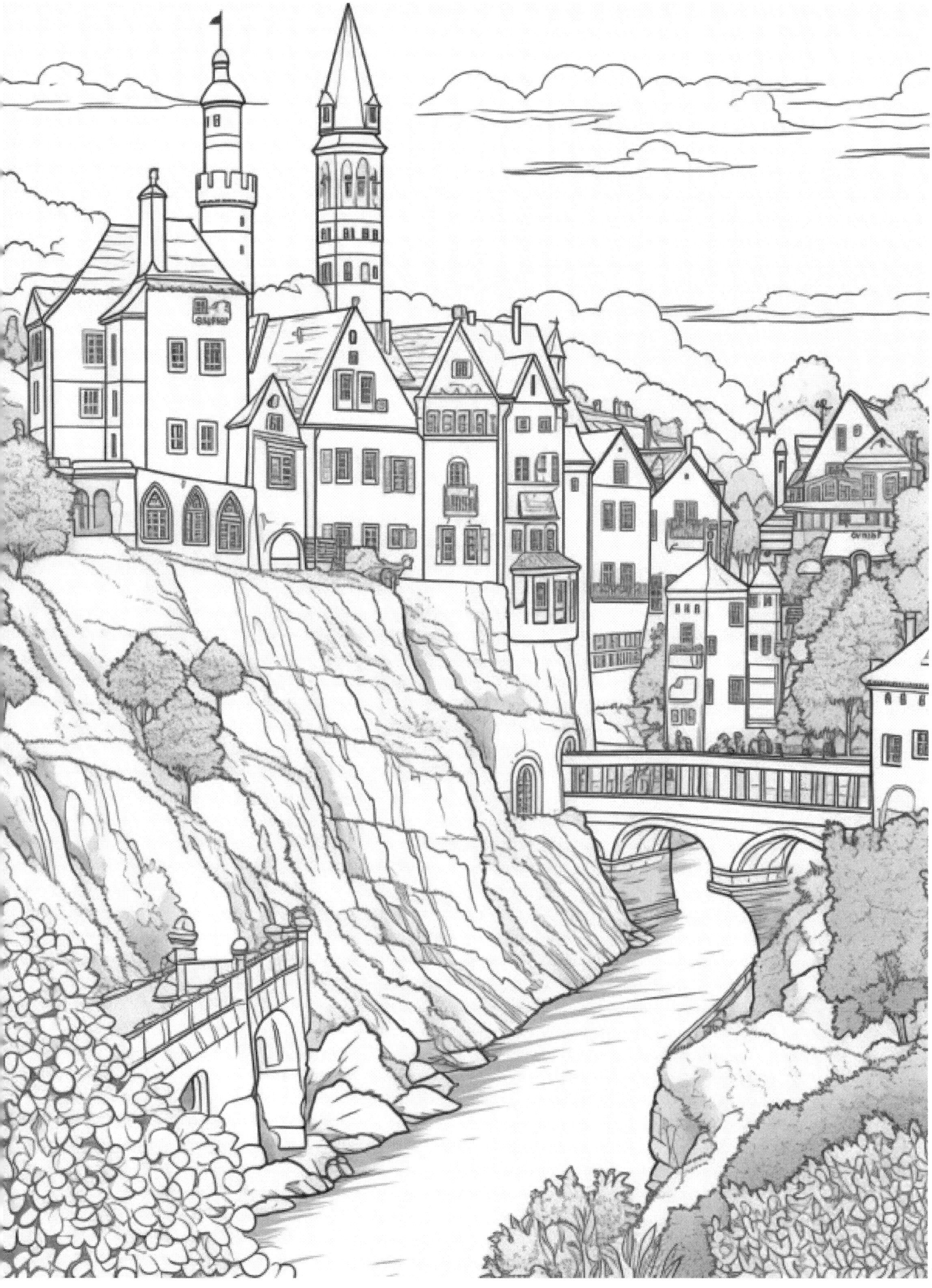

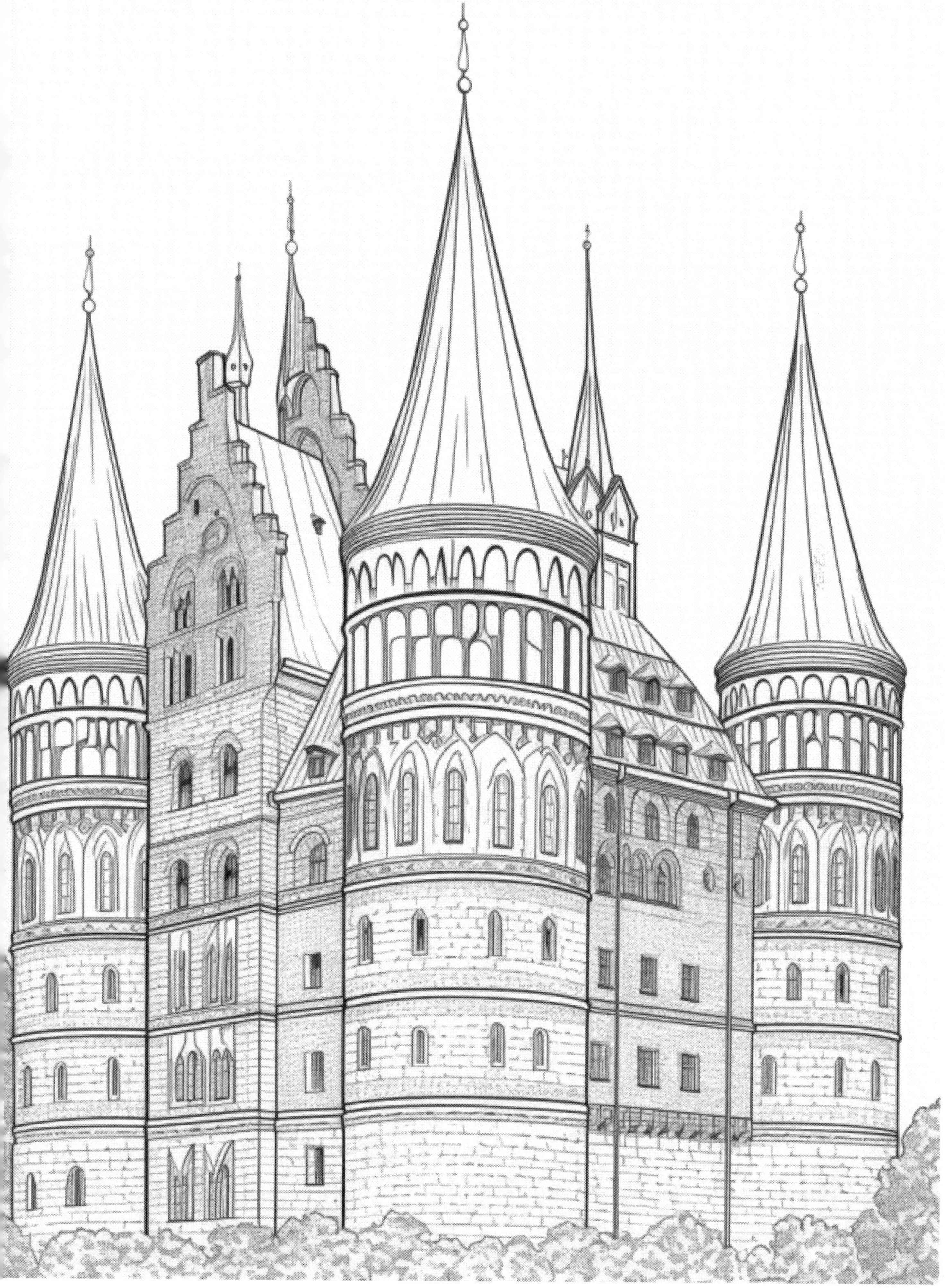

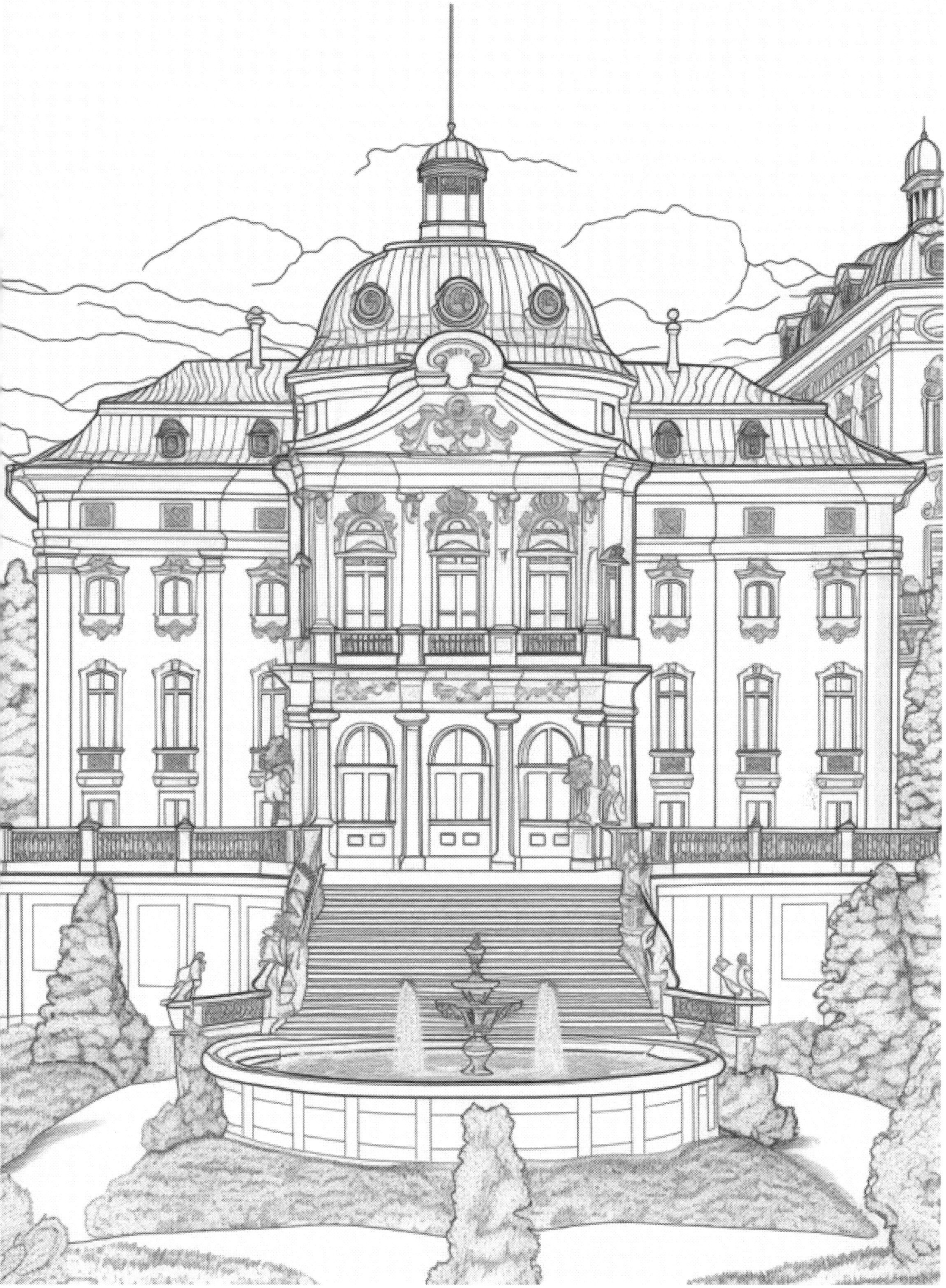

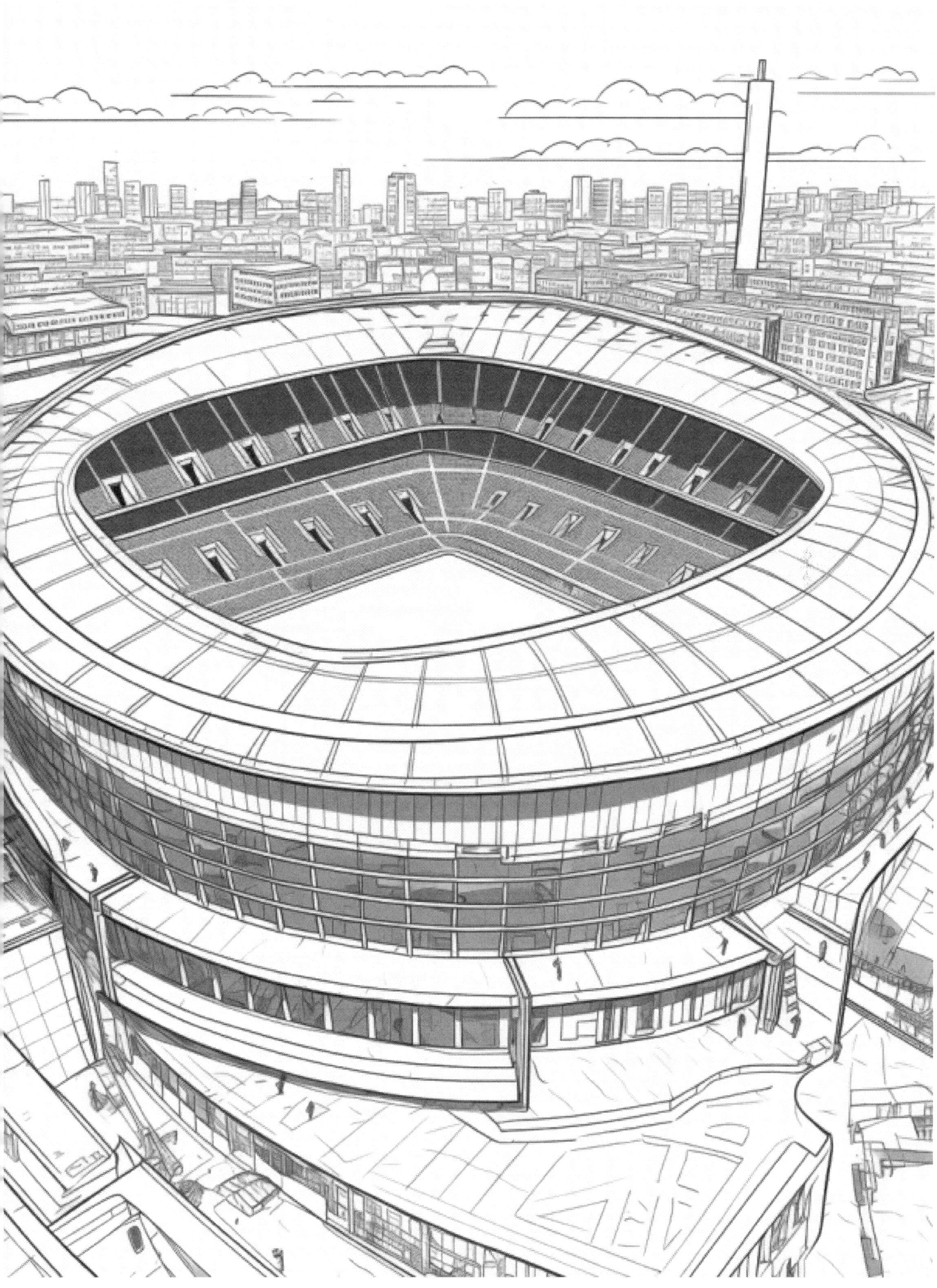

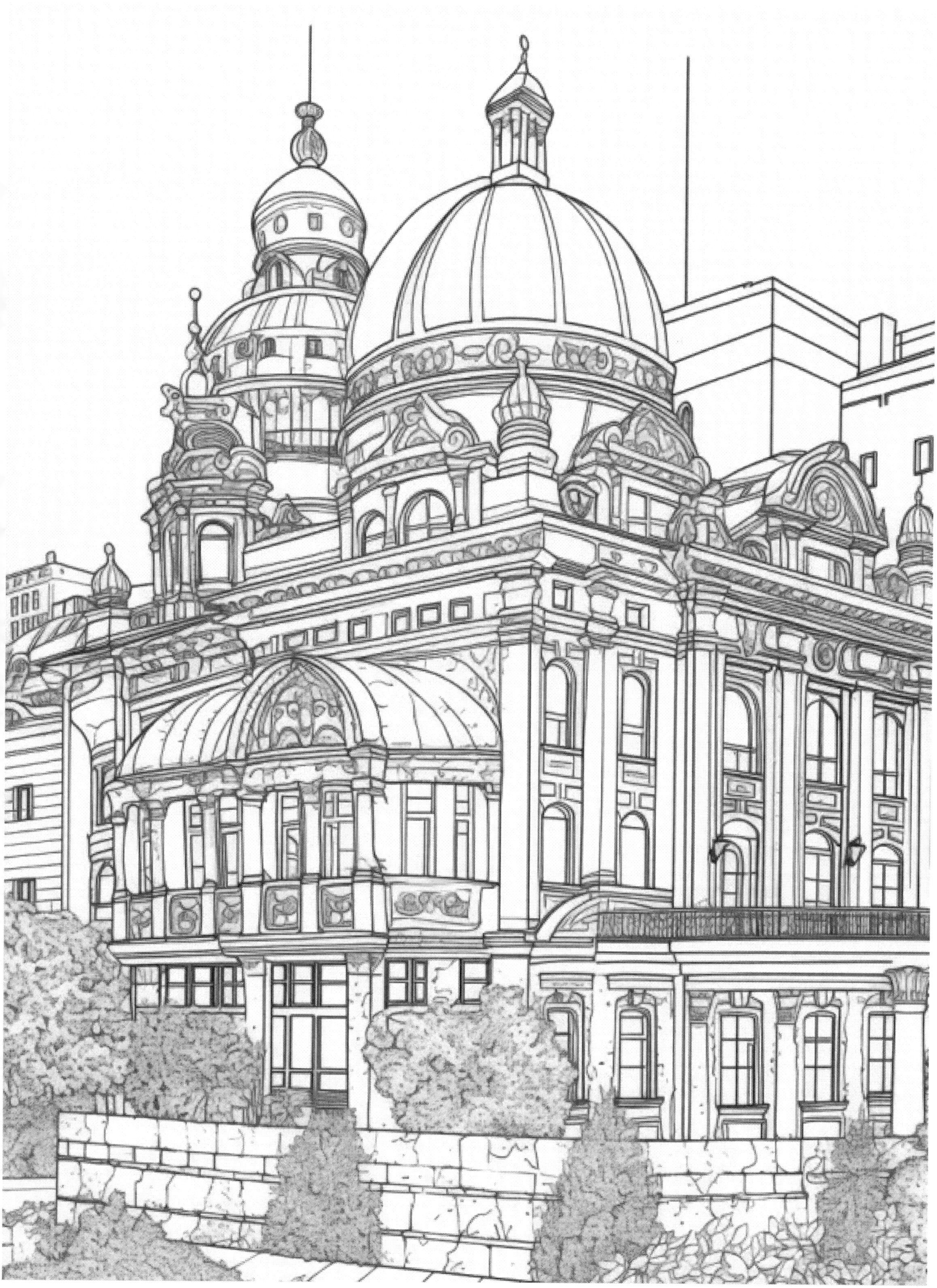

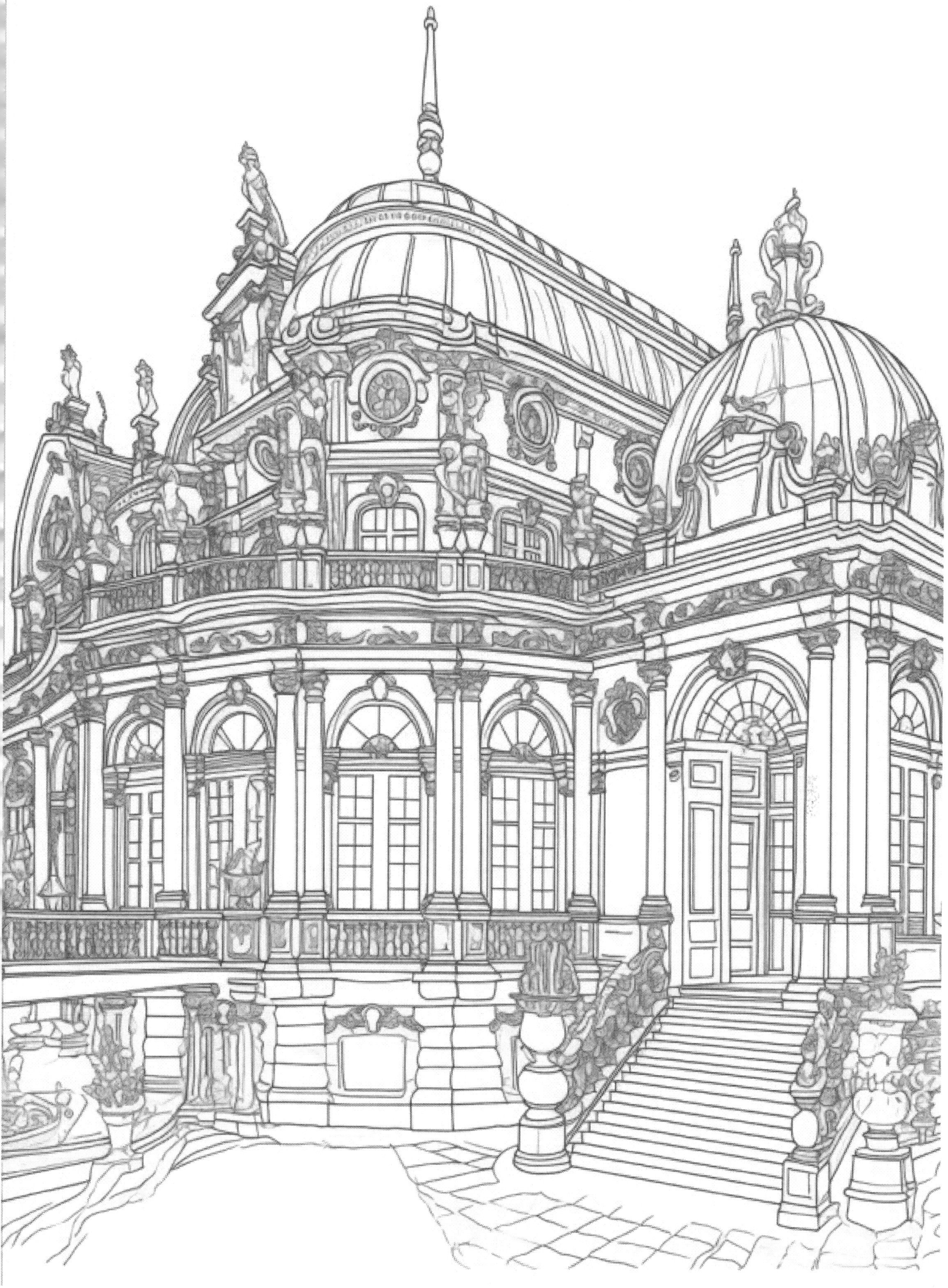

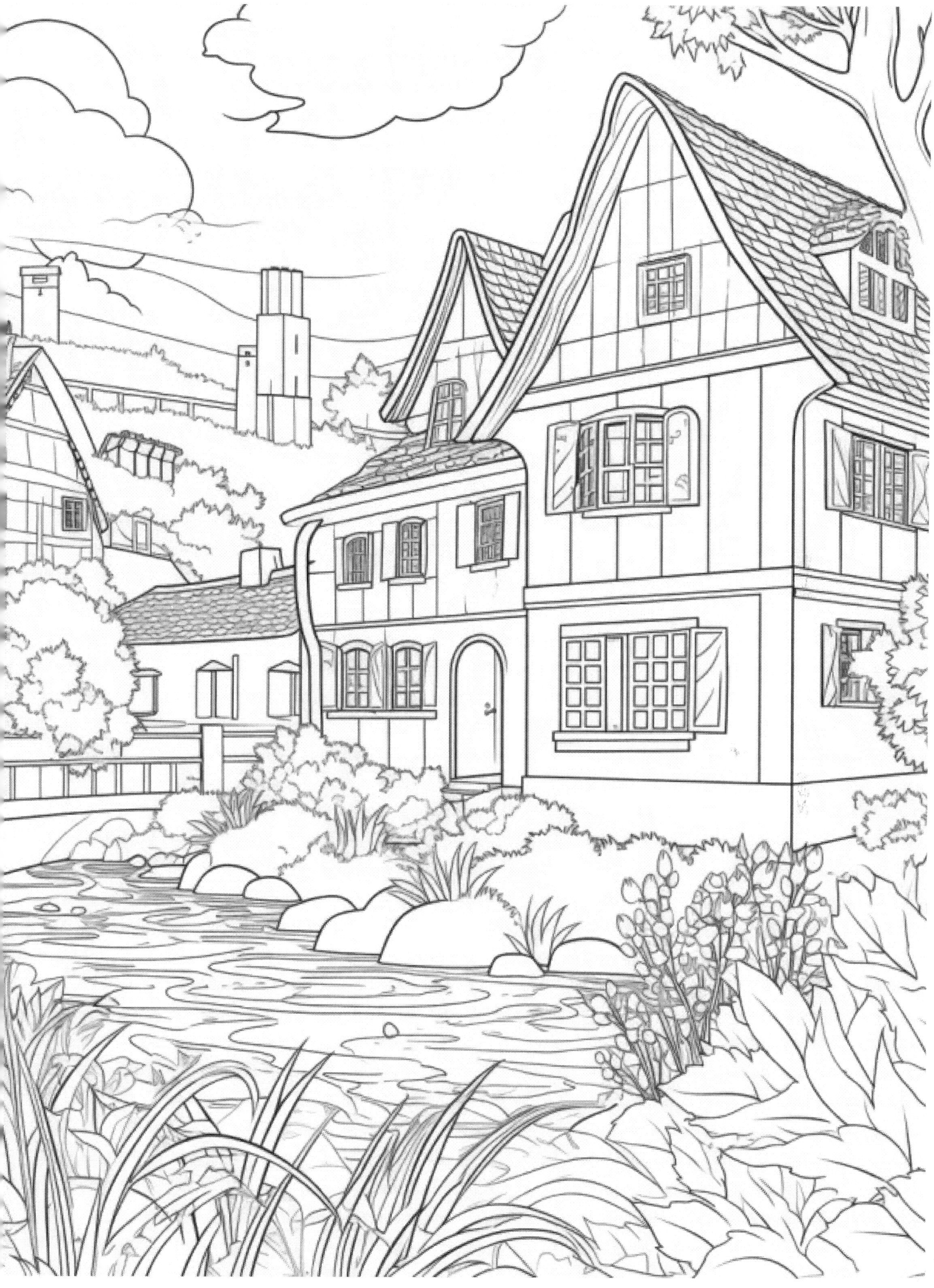

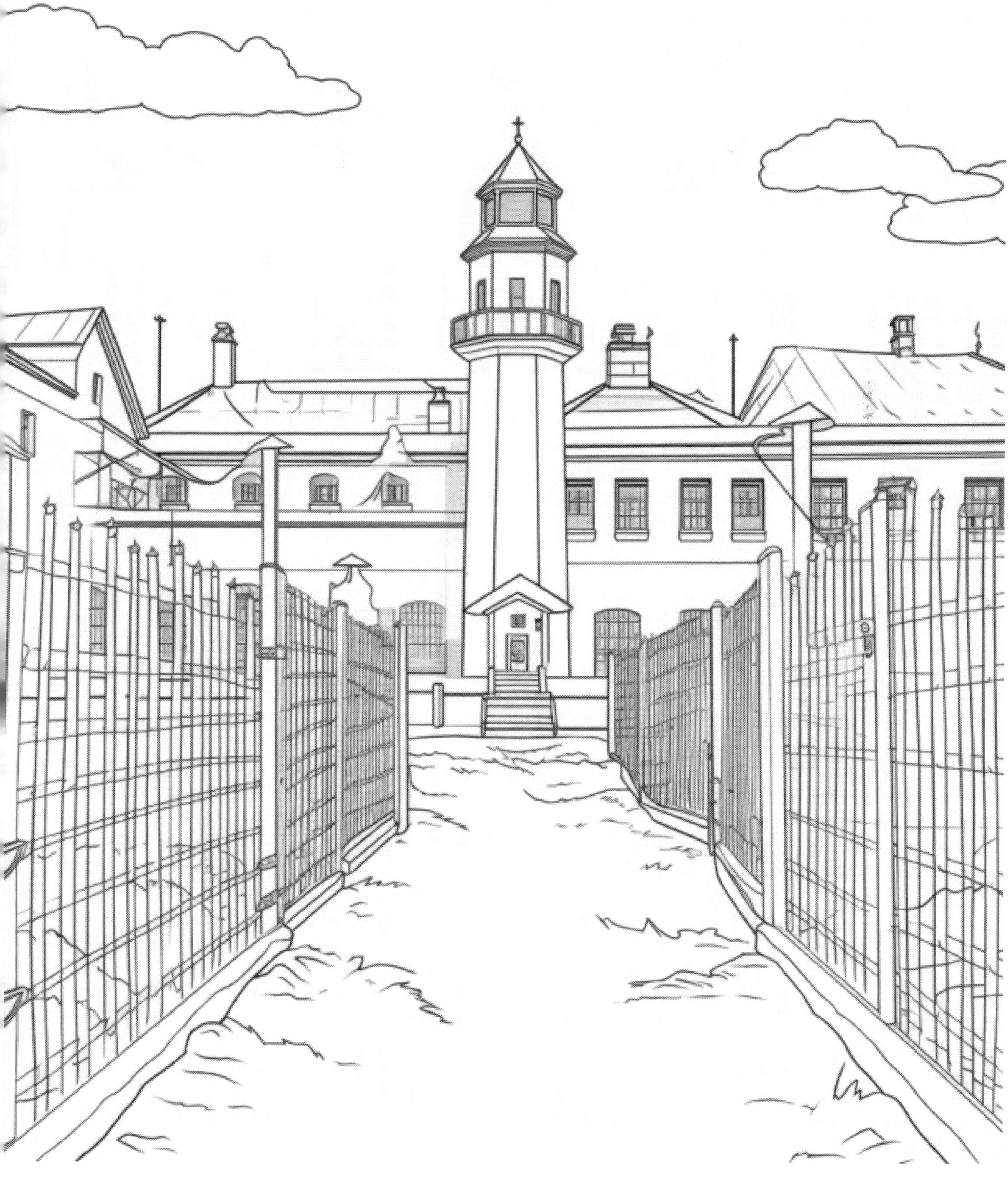

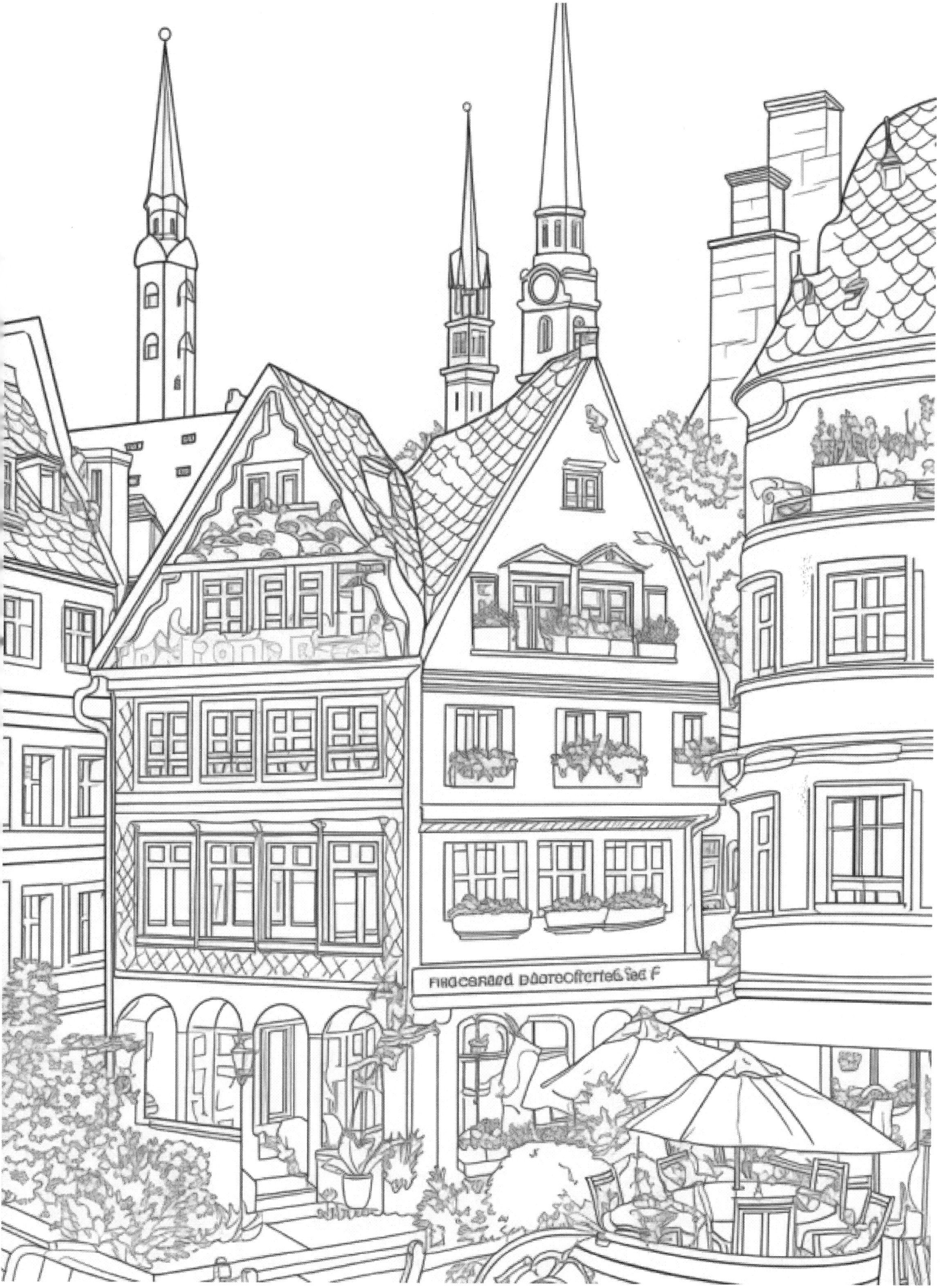

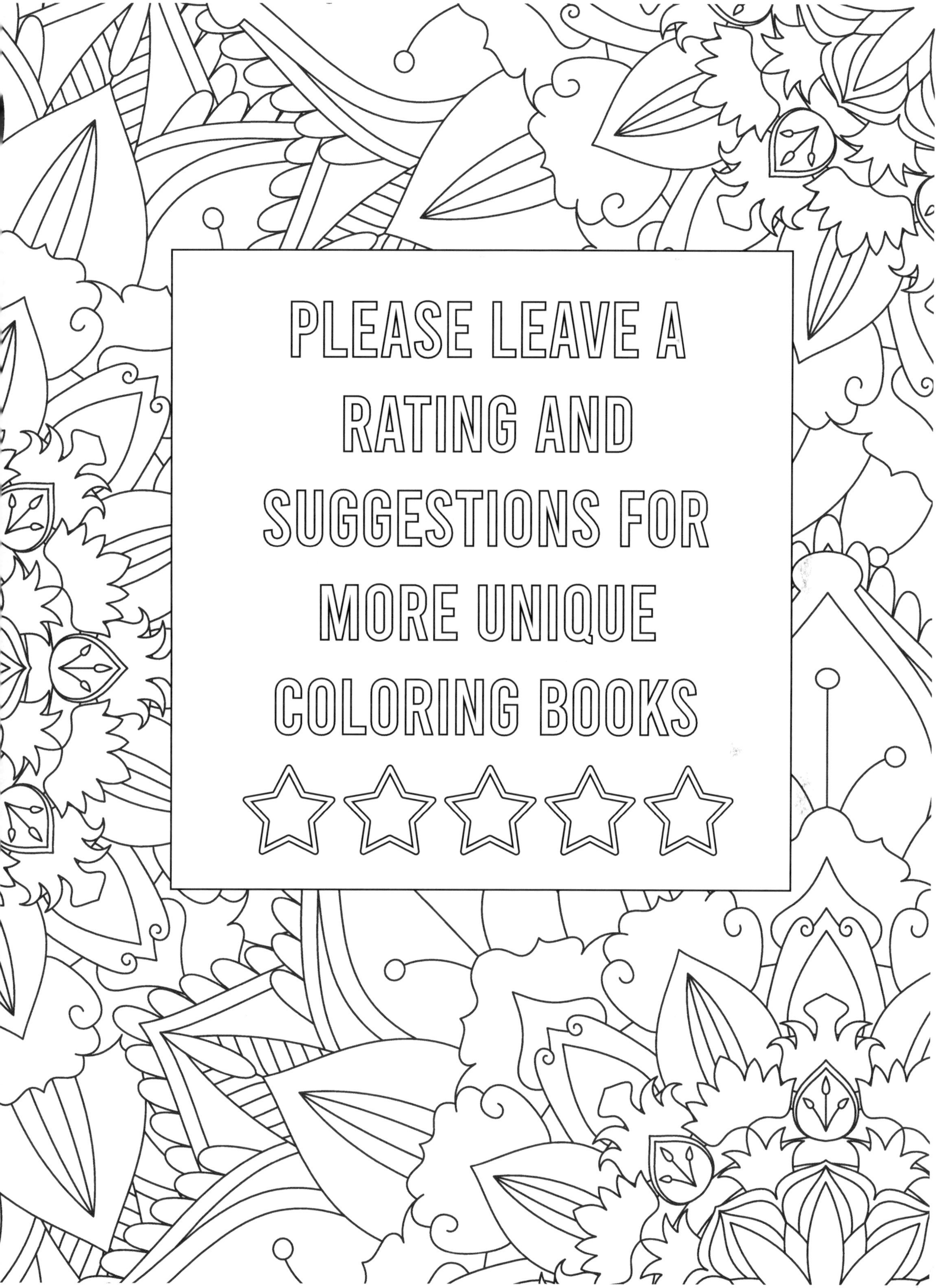
PLEASE LEAVE A
RATING AND
SUGGESTIONS FOR
MORE UNIQUE
COLORING BOOKS

Made in United States
Orlando, FL
03 May 2024

46448670R00057